T0062965

Ari Sitas

Rough Music
Selected Poems
1989-2013

deep south

Poetry books and manuscripts by Ari Sitas

Tropical Scars (Johannesburg: Congress of South African Writers, 1989)

Songs, Shoeshine and Piano in *Essential Things*, edited by Andries W. Oliphant. (Johannesburg: Congress of South African Writers, 1992)

Slave Trades (Grahamstown: Deep South, 2000)

Rhythmskewed (unpublished, 2000) – translation of a manuscript of 1991 Greek poems in Cypriot dialect

The RDP Poems (Madiba Press, Durban, 2004)

The Book of Accounting (unpublished, 2008)

Insurrections (CD + booklet, Centre for Humanities Research, University of the Western Cape, 2012)

80 Days Around the World – the India Section (forthcoming 2014)

The Vespa Diaries (under construction)

Poems from unpublished manuscripts have appeared in *New Coin, Badilisha Poetry Exchange, The Common* [USA], and *Marikana. A Moment in Time* edited by Raphael d'Abdon.

2013 © Ari Sitas
All rights reserved

ISBN: 978-0-9870282-2-8
ebook ISBN: 978-1-928476-18-4

Deep South
contact@deepsouth.co.za
www.deepsouth.co.za

Distributed in South Africa by
University of KwaZulu-Natal Press
www.ukznpress.co.za

Distributed worldwide by
African Books Collective
PO Box 721, Oxford, OX1 9EN, UK
www.africanbookscollective.com/publishers/deep-south

Cover and section page design: Adrie le Roux & Elmarie Costandius
Text design: Liz Gowans

Contents

from **Tropical Scars** (1989)

    Ethekwini 9
    We Continue 11
    Doubts 15
    Our little tropical scars 16
    Evening tides 19

from **Songs, Shoeshine and Piano** (1992)

    Shrieks 23
    Shantytown 24
    Crooning 25
    Mango Tango 27
    Washing 29
    The Monkey-Tree 31
    Barbarism 34

from **Slave Trades** (2000) 39

from **Rhythmskewed** (2000) originally in Greek, 1991 63

from **The RDP Poems** (2004)

    Black Mamba Rising 73
    Reconstruction 77
    Living Rites 82
    Times of deliverance 87
    Lament for the Dying of the Word 90
    Bombing Iraq 94
    RDP Film Documentary (RDP Project Launch, Inanda 1995) 107

from **The Book of Accounting** (2008)

    Summer Love 113
    Jazz, Bass and Land 118

from **80 Days Around the World – the India Section** (2010)

Mooring 123
Master and Slave Dialectics 125
Learning to Love 128
Remembering Freiburg..130
Allahabad 132
Varanasi 134
Kolkata 2 135
Kokovoko...137

from **Insurrections** (2012)

Ghosts of the Quarry: Insurrection 143
Insurrection: Flowers 144
The Eighth Insurrection of the cow 146

from **The Vespa Diaries**

Klerksdorp 151
Evening Song (Durban)...154
Marikana..156

from **Tropical Scars** (1989)

Ethekwini

There is
    an expanse of green and dust
    hemmed-in
        by cane and a stitchwork of hills
there, here,
   this expanse
      spat at by waves
      pummelled by sunblasts
        stewing in sweat
        yes, liquid
        yes, waves: whose necks are
        thickset with corrugations
there, here
    is this expanse that claims me: my Hell.

From here
    from this hell's odours
      – tomato street, guava avenue, molasses valley
      steel-shavings township, glue location, masala hill
        melting and boiling–
  there is no stench of heaven left to prize
      there is a sky: yes –
        blue-like, grey-like, alien-like
          weighing downwards
           pouring
            sweat
             at dusk
              downwards
          riveting all aground
         downwards, yes –
        with only sideward escapades.
There, here,
    mechanical bullfrogs and cicadas grind away
     and sometimes wounded cars cough-by pierced by
assegais
     and sometimes surfers emerge from the mouths
  of microwave ovens

and aways
life continues like the sound of splintering glass.
This hell,
        hemmed-in:
                its forced geometry of concrete boils
                spreads outwards
                        sidewards
                                in its rashes of sackcloth
                                of shack, of specification matchbox
                                to touch the stitchwork of hills
                        as near the docks
                                the boss drives by in his Shepstone Benz
                                as his "boys" load Cetshwayo's skull as
                                cargo
here, there,
        confined
                where visions of heaven subsided long ago
                with the arrival of sails creaking
                        under a hyperload of sparrows

here,
    there,
            in this maze of splintering glass
                in this expanse that claims me
                    in these infernal flamewaves tanning my fate
                    I was lost there
                        smiling
                                porcelain smiles
                    and waving
                            ox-hide kites.

We Continue

"WE ARE"
we said
    fingertips touching
    and
      "we SHALL BE"

We stood
    proud
     fencing-up
       channels of sound
        "we ARE"
        we used to bellow, strutting,
         and, "we SHALL BE"

then unexpected
     tearing the fences
        cracking through
        cracking-in
        arrived a time of grief
        and of assassinations
rusty-coloured Fiats
        stalked the gate
       and there were messages and signs
        that we OUGHT not
        and that we WERE not to be.

but then
    unannounced
       tearing
        came nights of pain:
         torn-lung
           morphine nights
          orange nights
            torn-bellow nights
            bare-lamp aglow nights
           nights of shreds
          as the impis were marching
            in KwaMashu

and then
              came spasms
              and the memory of harbour light – to the left
              Marine Parade – to the right
              as that breathless orange night
                  was downpressing
                      down-downpressing
                          to palpitation
              from Addington's rhythm and blues
                          and surgical scissors
                  and look:
          my junkie friend
                  complained once more of a dud dosage
                  nurse: "nurse, nurse,...Please,"
                  clawing his clock
                  scratching at the passage of hours
      as the impis marched out of KwaMashu
              with Bambatha's head on a stake

and of course,
          through those orange hours
              of half-delirium
          I was found
      crafting lovelorn jingles like
          "yes there you are
              searching for love you are you are
              searching for love you are"
          and I sculpted
              little devils drumming toyland hoofs
              and I dreamt of them
                  ejaculating birdshot
      as the impis marched through Imbali

and of course there was a maze of pain:
              morphine, doloxene-nights
              a writhing snake
                  with card-sharps and sailors
                  as Dube high school was raining stone

and there amongst the gangsters ploughing
    Point road alleys
and alcoholics – their liver in a newspaper
              under their arm –
driven by the cranes to yellow oblivion
as the yellow combis roam hunting
for calves to cull...
stitched mouths and livers squawking
bellowing laments for some lost wife:
"and where are you now, where are you now
  cause of my tears"
and I crackling:
"searching for love you are you are
   searching for love you are"
as the miner in the room is looking for his lost abdomen
   under the beds
      lamenting his hate for lahnee sports like cricket
   and the tattooed fitter and turner in the ward
bending over the basin in search of his lung
apparently spat out by mistake
as the streets of Kwamakhuta and Makabeni are also orange
aglow
and the merchant marine gentleman
is tied to his chair, amnesiac and connected
to a world of emphysema pumps
and there they are:
the lovers: she, with leukemia dying
he, 18, injecting mercury up the veins to join her
as we go spinning and bubbling
in this laboratory of pain
as this red bull of Mahlabatini
the martial eagle, blood on his claws
the eagle –
   who received the son of Ndaba's blessing
      the eagle who received Luthuli's mantle
and who soiled it in blood
the commander of vultures
roamed by

and I shouted
    from this glass tube
    that we are trying to be
    and that most certainly we shall be
        ever-present
            observing this cataclysm of tears

we have been
    silenced as teller of tales
    for only brief times
        but again we are starting to crackle

"we ARE"
  and "we SHALL BE heard"
      we say,
          and we add
"we were bequeathed
            to loudhailer lives
                and so we are condemned to crackle
forward
                                on and on and on"

we do

    through these nitroglycerine nights
        we do through these orange nights
            convinced of the red ochre of dawn
we do
    continue
we do.

Doubts

And I, Kurtz?
– with what
        With what skulls
do I adorn this firmament of light?
With shimmering bodies spliced on cable wires?
electrodes suspended
from
      imploded nerve-ends?
Eyes spliced in the grids of my jungle?

And I, Kurtz?
– with what I ask
        With what skulls
do I adorn this firmament of light?
With my wincing at the mention of pearls?
With my horrors
          at the mention of necklaces
my friends make daily
at Dunlop's?

Our little tropical scars

Night parades people on the promenande
      But in the narrow streets skirting the fanfare: howls.
Oh yes sister,
        I heard them and registered intensely
I, fumbling-through,
          a drydock mariner restless:
listening and on drunken night playing the sailor from Tangiers
entering your life, tattooing mirrors
           and was gone
with the room spinning around your disconnected fan
  scrambling-out in the maze of palm, of pine of plastic
with all this texture spinning
and inviting me
to the whiskeyed life of a decade
torn down there, unconscious of the unprostituted
lives upon the hill
eager to make a bookladder to the top and
   page by page to climb there

And I was told that —
From the hill my dear on a clear day you can see the class
struggle forever
on the hill my dear
     lives get caught in these damp afternoons
       and it's too hot my dear to read Frantz Fanon
     you are condemned to consume
to suffer the melancholy stalking of shopping-malls
  but to consume in taste nevertheless
skating past the torpor of palm trees and video vistas.
My dear Zigmund Gumede
I bring you these tropical scars
an overripe mango
  bruise marks   scars   sensations
and feelings and stitches and eina...
each day a fingernail scrapes off the miniscule scabs
I bring you these tiny, our little tropical scars
and you speak of the fragrance

of summer afternoons
and it hurts.

The valley rattles its nighttrains like springs
and we lay
listening to prerecorded love-sighs
there is no love left in the city
there are trees
bowing down
in their humble obedience of storms
there are people
felled
the dawn's street cleaners sweeping leaves and dreams
and eina...the sun arrives
in shorts and boxing-gloves.

Cartoons: yes, cartoons
a city of commix and shuffle
eim gonna twisja nose, twist-twist
eim gonna boink joface, boinkoboink
eim gonna poo-pooh your therapist
ja what?
jaa whaat?
but dear Zigmund Gumede when I say good morning to
myself the mirror scowls back, and I have this need to
express myself, good morning how am I, and to learn to
adjust to this cruel, this, this, this. Eim gonna poo-pooh
you therapist if you gonna boinkoboink my face.
And the sun shines in shorts and pummels with boxing
– gloves, over and under tko.

Dear Zigmund Gumede
and they say from the hill on a clear day we can see the
class struggle forever
but how? all we see is this mirror
          the scowl
and we bring you our tiny tropical scars
to crochet around them a meaning
to let us possess a large enough meaning

to cover the cracks
good morning how am I dear Zigmund Gumede

And I looked down the hill
a film of mist
spliced-through by factory chimneys
and the mirrors and sun rays reflected spiked at my eyes
and I looked at my bookladder
page after page soaking in sweat
and I tore out a page and fashioned a wing
and I tore out one more to fashion another
and I took my gadgets and roughed up my hair
and drew myself an overextended Might Mouse tail
and I flapped off the precipice
in search of the swamps
down below
to gather mud-words
to mould again
dreams of slime.

Evening tides

When the sun sets behind KwaMashu and further back
past the thousands of hills
and the cattle are herded
and the children are rustled inside
and the mothers count them again removing
thorns, lice, birdshot
with caring hand

and we feel alongside our shoulders making sure that our head
still weighs our neck down right through our spine
and the descending grey disappears the sharkfin,
the boatyard, the casspir
we are left with only our fiercer loves
and the sounds of hooks that we tear out
from each other's hearts.

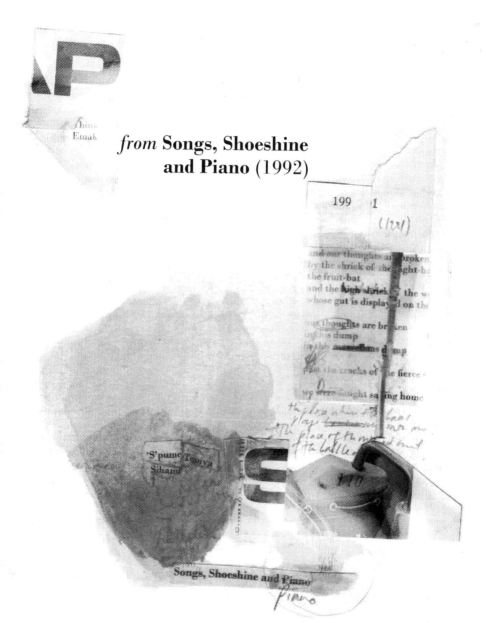

from **Songs, Shoeshine
and Piano** (1992)

Shrieks

Our thoughts speed-by the cracks of the fierce wind
and the waves crashing the stern
scrambling our brains
they speed-by the timber-furrows left open by Dias
to rest at the place where the half-slave knelt
where the half-slave cried about his karma
in the place of the monkey, the serpent, the gun

the place where the baas plays lambkin come unto me
the place of the mixed-root
of the babble of scripture
and Allah and Jesus and Krishna
and hallellujah the abalozi are not coming home
marking the start of the difecane of the brain

and our thoughts are broken
by the shriek of the night-bat
the fruit-bat
and the high shriek of the woman
whose gut is displayed on the tip of spears

our thoughts are broken
in this dump
in this marvellous dump

past the cracks of the fierce wind

we were caught sailing home

'S'pume Topiya
Sihamba ngomoya
Thina solala
Emakhaya'

Shantytown

The earth has crusted hard
and all thousand little feelings
have stiffened into structures
ejaculations, harsh, distinct
without form, crude, scattered eyesores
each one a little economy of hunger
each one loud, aggressive
this space is singularly mine
my rags this side
that side, thine.

Stiff tips press down the chords
my right thumb pulls a string
my fingers pluck my echo chambers loud
hat skews the eyesights
lids tick off flies
that sun squeezes out my cheeks until they water
neck strains so you can trace the words
they travel up the windpipes to the skies
this space is singularly mine
my rags this side
that side, thine.

This song has hardened like a hide
like our collective skin
stretched out for you to drum onto it a stick of fury
stretched over like a tent to stop and catch the rain
softened at night to tremble with these simple hearts
with sighs,
to feel the scraping of that corrugated tin
this song has strained its patience to its tether
cardboard, asbestos guttering and twine
my rags this side
on that side, thine.

Crooning

We hurt from the lives we will never live, those better
lives, those lives ELSEWHERE
We go dying each day a little bit more, drunk from the
shame we inhale
flattened here, we go dreaming of invisible lungs balloon-
pump-upping our threadbare skins
we go spooning-in here the filth of this city, meekly
smiling and escaping too soon into the alleys

    to croon
          we go crooning:
          sink into the hour, the twilight hour
          devour the night
          guydoll, jellyroll your spite away

Father worked across the bay where they used to cut
blubber and meatpacks from whales
I swear to his last his hands sweated-out codliver oil and
on his last our lives started sinking
and me, his little ground-sailor with my Sunday blue and
white collar and hat entered the fishlife
the payroll of bones, the hurt of the other side, the
wrong side the crusted beard salt-life apprenticed

    to croon
          we go crooning:
          sink into the hour, the twilight hour
          devour the night
          guydoll, jellyroll your spite away

I weep for the mermaid, tattooed or eaten added tuna
and parsley or admired on the porthole's mouth
We hope as we moan, as we stir in the murk, in the
voodoo rites of factory pots and pans and molasses
we despair of the lies of the other life and tear open all
angels reading their innards for signs

we snap-off wings and we start flapping and pacing
about incanting our lost years and speed-off

      to croon
              we go crooning:
              sink into the hour, the twilight hour
              devour the night
              guydoll, jellyroll your spite away

We hurt from the lives we will never live, those better
lives, those lives ELSEWHERE

Mango Tango

We used to dance the toyi-toyi
and then from France there came tua-tua
and then came tropical fruit from joburg
some people there do the guava juice: 'quattah!'
we here, we do the mango...tango

after the grinding day
I strut out
marching a two-step, a two-step, leap and block
groaning about
and then I tap my sole, tap my soul
and spring a two-step, leap, a two-step, leap we go.

I am dancing look twisting to the end of time
I am dancing look this road is mine
I am blasting till the walls of Jericho fall
I am dancing past verwoerd,vorster, botha their friends
and all

I am leaping look I am the egret shooting thru the sky
I am the eland
the hippo
I am the casspir-catcher fly

I am water
I am the waterfall
the downpour
I am the spark of all
them gone and coming back to life

after the grinding day
I strut out
marching a two-step, leap, a two-step, leap and block
groaning about
and then I tap my sole, tap my soul
and spring a two-step, peal, a two-step, leap and go.

We used to dance the toyi-toyi
but then from France came tua-tua
and from then on came tropical fruit from joburg
some people there do the guava juice: 'quattah!'
we here, we do the mango…tango

Washing

We went down to the river
– where the dhobis used to pound
their linen with stones
where the squatter-camp people
relieved themselves before
they were removed
where our children fished –
to wash the stains from our shirts

– each stain a memory
each memory: history unstuck, chasing the ocean,
tearing down our washing-lines

we cupped our hands and drank the muddy water
as the sun scraped at our tissue
and the shirts' threading tore at our fingernails
and we scrubbed
and when they washed off
we saw our years rinse down the banks
and we cried
and when they didn't
we cried
– each stain a memory
each memory a friend

and we closed our eyes against the glare and the light
and we prayed for the monster-wave, the monster-tidal-
wave, the largest wave, larger than all known waves, we
prayed to some seagod to stir up this wave, to gather
the lost, the dumb, the departed worlds from the seabed
and thrust them upstream back into life;
to gather the stains, and please,
remake back the loved ones and
place them upstream

we cupped our hands and drank the muddy water
we felt other hands, cut off,

severed hands coming downstream
and we lied they were logs
and their nails were as stiff as ours
in this monsoon time, floodtime
of our laundry days
we went down to the river
to wash the stains from our shirts
each stain a memory
each memory a friend
we felt our tired hands
departing with the others downstream
it was only our hands.

The Monkey-Tree

We are plucking out the the fires and our arms
are scabbed
the healing of wounds has been proclaimed

So we sit dear friend under the monkey-tree again –
have a pawpaw
the war has ended
let's go shoeshine and piano
we go

when the monkeys come
the dogs go yaowling
when the monkeys come you go
come
under the monkey-tree
again
my friend
let's talk
and then shoeshine and piano
we go

we used to laugh and throw stones
and flap about dancing, left foot up and, then the right
and listen to our visions on your box of wires
under our tree
we used to say we need a new kind of tree
to nestle our passions
like a palm with its obscene genitals at bloom
and better, a paw-paw pole added to feed our tribes
and thick tarzan ropes to swing from and bellow

and broad enough to hang a hammock
to sway our sherrywined heads
and space to leap left foot up and, then the right
and this we called our 'monkey-tree'
our mast our rudder and off we go

sugar and spice and spike
shoeshine and piano we go

and we sit here again after so many short years
so have a pawpaw
feel its bark now

and now, when the eastern storms excite the birds
and in spring
when the pollen and scent
make you scratch, or sneeze or cry
there is fear in the air
and then the monkeys return
drunk from all the perfume
and the first crescent moon
distorts all the people
     (there are horrid people near the sugar silos
     don't you go there at night
     all sugar sending places are hot
     all hot places have perfumed and rugged crowds
     and those who peg do not return to haunt you
     and if they do you can't remember them at all
     so they make futile noises just to scare you
     and then the monkeys return drunk
     and you forget them
     and you shake the tree
     and they show you their backsides
     and you tremble inside
     and you go)
come

then umngani wami, I must tell you
everynight at around sleeptime these four women come
out in dark saris and wail
     they send shakedowns down the spines of dogs and
     humans scuttle to hide behind their comforts
they could be singing an ancient lovesong of course
but no one cares
pain is pain

scabs are scabs
they will surely be silenced, don't go

Umngani wami, stay, it's safe here these days
I gathered your toenails and the expulsions that grow
through your scalp like hair
and mixed out of it the most potent brews
so you're safe
don't go
help me
to gather my memory that scattered
there were hairdresser of librarian,
they had plaits
they started blonde in my dreams but turned to
orange

and I remember holding orange tufts
in my teeth and my outstretched hand
and I remember in my pocket: baboon livers and teeth.

Something happened when they tore at
the sun's roots
and carved things out of its bark
and its sap was sweat or cancer

shoeshine and piano we go
in with the burrowing termites we go
come
there's peace at last.

Barbarism

It hurts to lose a dream – to live with the horror that
there will be no tomorrow better than our yesteryear
and our time to be marked only by this century's
register of gassed lung.

It hurts to lose a dream – we huddled in fear didn't we
up against each other, hair against hardsoft skin and
each footstep tapping the street sounded like a comma,
in that era of hope

But we took heart to dance for fierce gods – danced
on the foreground, each nerve and gesture and voice
tore at their conscience, tumbled and twisted their
moods

Took heart to dance without Him – even with
crutches we clumped at the earth with our sticknails
and heaved to ho and forward we go past the
abandoned tortoise-shells scattered on the road

Too hurt from the race to pray to Him – that that god
was a good god a god that walked barefoot, a she-god, a
god that cried, that bled, that sprang off the nails

(I lost you and your promise of paradise before my first
dentures; the thereafter was postdated. I tried. I did not
give up lightly, without shudder, without pain; but I
prayed and prayed, you abandoned me early and I
prayed so hard, my eyelids so tight, tight, tight, my teeth
sunk into the opposite gums, and I worded my pleas and
my murmurs, fast, fast, fast, but you did nothing and
they marched my kin outside. I lost you in the din of the
sound that sounded like our demented neighbour
banging on his metal bath, and I murmured, please,
please, please let it be bath-bangs.

Later, I walked with cool brain past the venom people

used to die for you, cut others for you, love others for
you. I could not play Abraham or hero this creature's breathing
was the only worth we had.

I gathered furies formed by this lean and stretched hide,
perforated by visors and scanners and tinglings and tiny
liver blasts and much hair scratching for openings.

To live, then. It was written.

To write, then.

To fly, then, sail then, search then
but also to fight, then, another war
beyond despair
where a jaundiced moon turns dusk to yellow.
there: where people tear and struggle with their
dreams.)

Sandlime and iron make cities and add aluminium will
conjure up cars
but I walk
there: the redmoon again
        the ochre on our shirts
        the earth that is chucked at our mouh
        to chew again
        the shacklands reach out
        as far as the heart can feel

and I say once again, pointing a wearied finger, a finger
pointed by so many others so much better, perfecter
before, point it at this known world, this tired space,
this universe without dreams, this chaos of pain and say
once again, surely it is wrong to be fleeced, starved and
kicked just to feed our owner, our merchant, our
bigdadadaddy.

ot with our plough, or flower or heart

but with an axe

I will pray for you.

...ars that suspend his rage and
cannot let you wander forever,
les and antheims.

from **Slave Trades** (2000)

You must place a rope around your neck, rough-up your hair and
go onto your knees in front of his seat, and you must plead with our
Lord, our Father, to bring you back to life, back into our clans. I am
sure the years have softened his rage and the Lord has touched his
psyche, he cannot let you wander forever, a poor woman, amongst
hostile tribes and unbelievers. I will pray for you.

(Note from Theodora to Marta Haymanot, 1895)

I had them strap a seat and lift me up
my body swelling, rotting in the sun
and march me down the twisted, acrid paths
to take me down to sea.

They shall count us after the flood and we shall still be two
I thought
After the flood we shall be counted two by two
I thought
but deep inside I knew that Africa had all its wiser ways
and on the road, the bone and shrub cut deep inside my soul.

They shall count us one by one astride our lonely beds
or else they shall not find us when the counting starts
and we shall dwindle off with just our putrid breathing
and cut the landscape up
       not with our plough, or flower or heart
       but with an axe.

ᴧ

I saw him lifted up, his face – flabby, loose, distended
his songs long forgotten,
lost in the fevers of his infernal sorrows
and his shroud, lean, threadbare and his colonies of slaves
sinking in the mud
his dreams floating down, down towards the Red Sea
his soft parts pulped, reeking the foulest of desires
and his hide – only a fish's sheen
his sheen a fish's scent.
His hirelings buckled under his weight

edging forward
a funerary bulk
moving past the ostrich's, the camel's, darting, bluegrey eyes.

∿

The sea is full of bluebottles the sky's a necromancer
crabs are prancing past your beard hairs
wet ash has smeared your seafront lairs
the wind has whipped the sand in you like a demented dancer

∿

I remember most of all his hands, large, larger than language,
stubborn hands, sturdier than a Harari horse
and his spoor of stale garlic, of ever-reeking sweat
plastered up in perfume
and his flannel underwear, I do remember grimy and his eyes
darting out haunted by the steps of perky Arab boys

I remember his hands and the gift of whiteman's disease and
semen in my loins
and he laughed at me –
"you truly believe in God?" he used to tease
as he held on to twist my nipple
holding the writ that made me his

for eighty guns,
        between his legs

∿

I woke up to face another day in this house
I saw the ravages of our estate once too often
The chipped mortar, brick and of course as always, the ash
I walked over the trinkets and the cracked remnants
and urged to go to find one who could finally destroy
who could finally rebuild our house
for I was weak , weakened by the day

and they, oh those infernal "they", were many
I sold her off for eighty guns
and all the guns for sailors' cloth
And I walked off with the sail wrapped around my head
against the cruel sun.

There must be a trail, I said, leading out of this land
of infamy and barter – a road
friendly to shoe-leather or sail;
to leave, yes – not through the fancies and the landscapes
of the mind
to leave, yes – the fences of this reasonable world
and its iced thinkings
and the chattering of all its nimble poets
to bid a final farewell to this horrid rack
where my works dried out
from the harshness of your trading winds.

I am to leave this house,
this garden
I am to leave these words behind
and all their well-wrought meanings

I am to struggle to be mute again
I am to leave these lurid coastlines
Europe, Aden, Natal, Ithaca or more

ᔋ

The roadside curb was to be my bed, and my rucksack slanting
off a startip's point above, and the spinning sky my shelter and I
remember how my head wined and romantic felt her face,
become the moon during those indigo-tinted nights.

The birds of prey would tune my song the dovecote's crap my
aroma my tattered boot and lace would be my harp, to serenade
her yellow glow to comfort me against the dreads and spooks of
night-time.

41

Come closer you wenches I'd cry drunk come closer I'd sing, male
or female, come trample on all of my casks of woe it's for you I
make rhymes torn or frail it's for you, you pieces of mutton or
tripe that I strum at my leather and pretend to grow a feeling
more felt than a gruesome pustule.

Often at night on the grass by the roadside, I'd rest my head on
your hairy belly, on your moist skin to pierce my earlobe and
my hand on your thigh and the moonlight dribbling light on
the furrows of your back, your front, catching us guilty us, of
unclean compassions.

But then again the bird would tune my song, our minds would
crisscross desert sands, I'd sing of how I carried you along upon
my shoulders kissing your scented hands and saving the taste of
our skin inside my heart.

The roadside curb was to be my bed and the choirs of heaven my
echoes, — the angels, fat, obese, howling heavenly hymns in my
stupor, their jaws striking out as gross as the yelps of my beaten
but comradely dogs, as gross as my life was then, as gross as it is
now and out of kilter.

Come closer you wenches my dreams come closer.

∿

Come here, follow me past the markets of Abbi-Addi
past my ancestral homes
where the older gods stirred thunderclouds with vengeance
and where the new one hammered on wood is
guarded by shrill, austere monks and parchment
come, here, look at the footprints
and the marks all creatures formed as traces in the mud
here: come, the zebra stumped a hoof
and here: a lioness and cubs have littered
come, follow me down to the canyon's forked fingers
that point you down and shove you down to my valleys
look: left, the Semien range – pink, pink from all the snow

and the harsh sunrays of my ancestral gods and later,
as the sun sets you will see how it makes the clouds
around its nose look like dark clerical hats on fire
now red, now redder, now redfire-coloured

Slide down the little waterfall with me
the rainbow
in the trickle will not hurt you
here, run through the coffee garden
past the fruit-trees and the flowers
smell how my people cook the thick banana on open fires
look at these pomegranates, oranges, limes

come, let us run around the hiss there
past the songs, boys and girls intone
twist with me past the bank of the Taccuzze river
come, here, by the tall poplars
here, you see, some of the footprints stop
here is the clubbing ground
the dented skulls heaped up just there
are of the ones who
were too lame to make it to the sea
to fetch a price, come, follow me,
see how the weather made them, how it makes them shine

〜

I walked to the edge of the cliff overlooking the sea
the sand and dragging the cloth
that was to be my wedding shroud
around my naked torso
I tied it with a knot around my neck
and let it fly and billow against the wind
a soft wave and flap above this hardened crater
backflowing, prising me against the sky
flexed my hands and felt my fingers tingle
I placed my index one on my forbidden parts
the other over my heart
and caressed until my nose aimed at the only cloud

and my toe, outstretched, outstretched lifted off
my shroud my wing to meet it
my lifting my liftoff and outstretched some more
floating over this wretched coast
to find my solitary star

～

Give me the moon she said not knowing that I hated women and
their petted cages, their canaries and the lice they grew in their
marvellous rose gardens; I would have never reached for the
moon for her, for them

They never understood that deep inside the hues that the sun
makes to dazzle on the water, on the wave which is cut in twos
by my dream-armadas, by my brainfins of a shark, all my
images of them have been stark, maternal, barren.

She never understood that she paced around my house as
ornament and sphinx for others; and I was kind with my love
for her, I was kind with my affection and my counsel; but she,
frowned and despaired and when at night, after her first sobs
and prayers, trembling and pleas, after boiling the sea water for
drinking in this parched, desperate, nothing of a town, she spun
a web around our bed and I sunk into my purgatory year.

I did not treat her like all the others do to her own kind; I did
not call her savage, brute and lice-infested wench; I did not place
a chain around her neck and lead her down to market; to the
growls of the surrounding town and folk I made her the princess
of my sand-infested, cow-dung polished dorms.

I fought for silk and thread for her in every market; I traded
wines and grapes for ornamental gold; I unloaded camel hordes
of rifles for her chamber's sheets; I paid in kind for years to get
her taught the French ways, to hold her own. But she paced up
and down my inner courtyard like a demented whore.

I did not come to this godforsaken place to dream, I did come to kill the dream, there was too much of it over there and much of it too soon.

She will be gone with florins round her neck, back to her tribesmen.

She will be gone because I cannot make her mine, and through my doorstep or outside in this treeless dump, no one else will make her his no more.

She will be gone from the records of our life and those who will remember her have not even learnt her name.

She will walk the three rows of mudhouses to the port in the early morning and the wind will resand her footprints on the path.

She will be referred to as this girl who lived with him, almost his wife, for almost one year; this tall, slim, light-coloured beauty with her matted hair who did not succumb to the Mission School's grind, who wore him out; the stupid native, who lacked the intelligence to be his bride; damn it, yes the woman he abandoned because he chose the adventurer's and the corsair's life.

I looked at her and said: farewell Eva, go.

She looked at me and frowned, turned and let Africa's magnet tag her in, away and in, and into the landscape of all of my despairs.

I am the she, whose centre disappears
I am not
I am unwritten
unclassified
I am the last murmur of something older
than chattel or rifle

I am the dangerous she
unbaptised
exposed without purdah
uncircumcised
bought for guns, but unpriced
unsaved from the serpent
with too many odours to be formed by a magician's brush
unlineaged, suspended in memory
dispossessed of any line that roots me aground in the wind
ancient, not Evaed
Nobkhubulwana knows my name
Athena knows my black name
When I play my harp
sonnets kill like arrows:

"I saw them coming to my homestead crying
their bare breasts stiffened from fear
hide us, they begged
you can have a score of the best spotted cattle
do not let us be taken by your Christian friends
give us genitals and clothes so we can be seen
as weak men and tie our breasts down so our chests
feel just flat and wobbly
hide us and we will give you the very first yam crop
the dates and the nuts we have grown
let us be seen to be defective men
rather than women with active wombs
and loins that can squeeze out animals for branding
in the market of the believers"

I see him now, consumed against a crimson desert sky, beyond
hope or death returning to the eel-eating country of his birth. I
see my kin, shading their eyes with the guns my brother bought
in exchange for my firm backside.

And I scream at the scrawny birds of fate – I am the she they
cannot centre, I am the unshe of their nightmares, I am the
footstomping, ever flowering mother of my ever thirsting rib and
torso and wing.

～

I remember how the poor once
long long ago dared stand and holler
to be cut down by military sabres
to be strung on bayonets

we were the poor
and that was our ark
was our commune
was our funerary call

in the enchanted houses
women walked about
dreaming of swans
of romances
of sedentary loves
roses, guitars and poets

In the dark alleys
and army barracks
I ate my shame, my fate
in the grime
to write verses in blood

In the enchanted houses
they murdered hope
the word was cheated
of its slime and truth
and the maidens dreamt of serenades
and a pale sun over some icy floes

In the streets the stench
of the carts
unto dust unto dust
carting dreams, calloused hands
to the fire

I will be gone I said

hammered on a wooden cross
and let downstream to float
out of these rivers and into
the undisclosed lands
of some tropical scented
and topazed sea

The poor took to the street
and said in simple words
that their lives were not for barter
the sky rained lilies, diamonds
marrow, shrapnel, bone

Beyond the barricades – I shouted
beyond madness's border fenced in by words
to search for what was not
what was not meant to be
that was unmined, unyielded, unexploited
untranslated, irreverent and free

To find my stolen heart
to turn the world into a monstrous soul
to turn my soul into a gangrenous leg
to dream my visions of a brilliant port
to pain with every other soul that pains
to draft the one communal constitution
scratched on the skin
scalped by the brain – bled on a leaf, a page, a drum.

∿

Accept these offerings from a damned soul to your unselfish
heart. As you became my slave and your hands remade the world
I touched, your stare bewitched my nighttimes, slipping in and
out, a shadow in my many rooms. I conjured with my wand new
flowers, new estates and caravans travelling up and out to gather
meteors, suns and cosmic stars and all those diamonds that
hide behind the moon. Accept them please, these offerings of a
solitary, unhappy soul.

I would be fit, given the ugly wounds I carry in my mind, for
a colony of lepers, strutting around holding the slices we have
scratched from all our imperfections. You would be fit, given the
kindness that irradiates your simple needs and eyes, to be the
secret code of an erotic book, playing with swift abandon with
the grammar and the verbs of all desire. I would be fit to only
be the author of that charmed book's errors, its blots and faulty
spellings.

As your country, your climate and your relentless blue-flamed
suns turned my skin to leather and my hands to rasps and my
fingers into scalpels, accept the softest of all of my caresses. As
my cottons, silks and slender flannels, my perfumes and lathers
have turned your calloused life to elegance and grace strike me
with all the force of your pent-up affections. I would then use
my hardened hide to strum the spleen of this Habeshi harp.

You stand for me harsher than ashen colours mixed with the red
feathers of the morning's scrawny bird, a bird that croaks at me
without a name outside the window, and smile and jest. I would
be too, red in my mind and darker than my psyche's urge for
you, perhaps a shade of moss after the summer rains, after the
roar of crowds stoning a sedentary thief, but I cannot.

Your obedience is final, total, bought.

ᔕ

First came the low flying birds
spinning their restless twirls
prefigurings of cloud, then grunt
followed then, spears of fire
burning the trees' beards
slicing open the ponds and lakes
and His Word was water rushing
speeding a painting mass
off and over terrifying cliffs
throwing fish, logs, rocks, froth
stunning the cattle

seizing hearts

If my words with obvious gift net the furies
of the cosmos' wrath, then race me too with the bizarre power
to command the flushing out of their bazaar visions
with the Hawash, Taccuzze, my riotous rivers
to exorcise their bazaar madnesses
to flood like Sodom and Gomorrah
towns like Harar, Asmara, Entoto and Macale
to raise a flag for Zion

I have seen the sickness take a hold and clasp souls and squeeze
until bodies tremble
into the dance of their despairs and squeeze tight
until inside their heads a dance of Things
rattles up and down their brains
eyes flickering
and organs numb
when the town's banter starts
as the gates open to the chattering
of traders and their sums

I have seen the bazaar madness running through a hundred
talers for a horse and half of that for bottled morning dew and
the other for some desert crabs, and dew, new sold for eggs and
crabs for soldiers' sweat, and eggs for khedive smoke, and sweat,
new sold for human tongues and smoke for zebra tails, and
tongues for sand and sand for 45 rhythms on the lute, and zebra
tails, newly sold for orchids and rhythms out for forests, and a
forest patch, newly sold for a bazaar woman's blinded father and
orchids sold for hair. And then they rested.

And then they started: this gun for that hare, this hare for some
grass, some grass for a ship, some ship for a hymn, a hymn for a
house, a house for a murder, few bodies for stones.

Give me the power to flood the stalls and tear at the fleshy,
dampened scabs, the boxed palmtrees and the sacked falcon
beaks, the shredded cocks, the bottled tears, the piled up

seashells and the dying sundried river fish, the whites, the blacks, the weighed summers and the trapped voices, the gathering of bird skull, baboons, balloons, spice and cloth and Menelek's stolen lambs.

The world has gone flattened, mad, devoid of life, pregnant with Things.

∿

Love me, protect me and trust me he said; but I had to go, to flee and he didn't like it, like we don't like pacing around all places where love had died

Please come back to me, and I miss you and all such trifles were his romantic daily fare, pathetic as he fussed over every hint of me and cried and cried

Look I am kissing your letters, I am eating your rhymes, ironing your clothes, shining your moccasin shoes, combing your hair, I love you I said but I lied

I am me, me all yours, all you for me, all here, he shrieked, drunk, hysterical, refusing to accept that indeed he was dead, a nothing, a well that had dried

My white, black redwhite lover, bled back
be gone, stand back

I will be leaving your city, look at its kidneys, its shadows, look at its officers of the law with cardboard wings erected on their backs, look at their lives

Your whores with tin-haloes, obese from too much bile and food, look how they hang their garters off the moon, look at them rattle too, the noise you call love-music in your cruel hives

Look at your drain unclogging workmen look what cancers they pull off your rats hair, look at their handbones crumble, warp

and burn look at them circumcise themselves with their blunt
knives

My white, black, redwhite lover, bled black
be gone, stand back

I will leave the crumbling church wall far behind, your bourgeois
magic further still, your fetid smells and worn out suits, your
many tremors of the flesh and moans

I will not rest in some rural dale, with our pale sun adrift, alone,
lamenting the perfume of lost loves, the hazes that your voice
out-drones

be gone, stand back

I will be the dancer on a sea so thick, thicker than wine or a pond
so thickset and dark by a scented town so thirsty for my porous
exile so deep that it holds no memories of the drowned, the dead,
the slave, the knife, the black angel's versifiers so grey that it
forgets the sun. And You.

∿

Trees cry each time a bird lifts off
their limbs and hair
And I can not find comfort for
their bloodshot eyes
I can not dance for them
and they do not dance for me
they sing only with a hoarse voice
about the fruit they'll never bear

I was supposed to pluck another fruit
to force the door of Paradise to shut
forever, I was supposed to ire the
sentinels by burning the innards of a
beast on some ancestral pyre, but I did
not – I cursed instead the wild rose

and hurled its meanings and its perfume
in the fire

Trees cry each time a bird lifts off
their limbs and hair
Birds go to affect and haunt
Another melancholy dream.

∿

My heart is filled with joy at the news of my pardoning. In a few
months I will be there riding next to you for Zion. The time is
right for us to strike at the Italians. I hear that in the South, the
Kaffirs, Zulus and others are rebelling in the name of Zion and
that the children of the slaves in the Americas are calling out our
names. Here the real Christians are talking to the Russian ones to
find common cause against the Anglos and the Ottomans. I will
be boarding an Italian ship next month and will scale again our
Habeshi heights

(Haymanot to Ras Ailula, Lemesos, 1894)

The sea reddens twice,
each time the sun refracted by its face strikes at the dunes
and then in concert the dunes strike back to pluck
at lice-rays from its hair

There is a third, a man-made henna when the chattel
limp and useless is placed against the wave and scum
for the playful shadows – steel-plated lobsters of the deep
sharks whose muzzle whistles as they tug
the fish-choir with its chattering smiles and teeth
the seagulls, forests of angel wings descending, pissing up
against our song

The sea reddens twice, we sing
each time the sun refracted
the red sea, the Red Sea, boys,
the sun boys, the closer to him we fly
the colder the winds, boys, the dunes, the hair

to the south boys, turn our skewered, rotted hull
aim the rudder's soul towards the ice, ragged cliffs, spiked
beards boys, like a wounded aloe, our souls boys

Pray for Johanna
Saved by a she-whale, deposited inside her rounded gut
she sings, boys, each time the whale leaps
from the deep red soup to tease the rays
the sun-hair boys, red streaks boys
she sings from the whale's deep chamber
a muezzin voice against the prow, her
voice, boys, come to me she sings,
come free yourself, there are free tribes here
surging past the dunes of earth's
clay-shaped power, come

The sea reddens, twice, thrice
the Red Sea
the lice-rays teasing hair
the murmur of prayer
the chattel, Johanna, the memories of your pleated hair, sing
boys, sing, conjure a songwind
tear at the wave

∿

I snapped the chain that held the
wrist close to the hearth
and left the pot stirring itself upon the fire
and left the jugs go full themselves, Go I
said, jugs drown yourselves out there at the pond
the pond, immobile, calm, serene will cover you
with emeralds and weeds
and filter from the sun the kindest light
in time

I left the homestead empty, the rooms
strangely smeared in camomile scents
and the dark cisterns with residues of grease

and the landscape without a swan in sight
or a pensive horse tugging at the grass
that hides the world's dried vein
and ash and thyme
I shut the final window where
the childhood singing tones scraped in
and folded up the picture of the fig tree
of my youth, dancing and jumping at the pond's
far end, the swan pond
my pond
the corpse-less pond

Comb now I said your thinning hair
before your breasts sag and lose their shape
drape your fugitive cape across the setting sun
and learn to live

〜

We shall go
leave, we shall erase our stamen from history's
            favourite haunts
and colonise some territory that
ploughs for the seeds of dreaming

and in the dark
if you are wading through a field
of decaying bird, a calcified eagle
and scattered feather remember
that some seeds turn nasty
but most turn the spine of a
navigating star

We shall return
we shall arrive again in boats
            of shredded skin
and reclaim the land that
echoes still, the dream of seeding

I shall return to the desert's sands
when my wrist is loosened from the bolt
and the orchard's songchain abates forever

I have in my head the desert's hues of colour
its skies so blue, bluer than the deepest blue
and i see already the panther's footprint
in the sand
and the dream of flowers hovering over the dune
as I will run, nerve-taut, muscle-taut,
past the ghosts of burnt-out houses
and the madness of wandering souls

I have in my head the faint chill of the desert's moon
fainter still, as the sand whizzes and stirs
and the moon's jaw-line whispering the secret
meanings of rain, the clues to the soul of the heavenly
cistern and the spread
of dead roots clutching at the neck of its arc

I shall return to the sands with a camel
camels patiently nudge at the horizon, step over step
because camels do not dream
they nudge and nudge
caressing each other's necks
and stare at our pain with their eternally-sad eyes

I shall find in the desert's sands
the mucus-ed milk of our despair
and the wisdom of wind-carved stones
and I shall enter the harsh estate
the pyre which will burn our soul
and will spread my holiness like a garment of gold
and help the skin ashine against our bone
and feel its deserving pollen
its fragrance from the end of time

~

Wring your hands at the doorstep
avoid to stare
and shift your weight from one foot to the other
search your pocket
and uncrease your wares gently towards their sights
your next move is vital
do not pretend you already know that you will be sent away
give them the magnitude of the moment they deserve
and when they point you off
remember: the cities that have claimed you
are ashed.

~

These evil times, autumn already
with the sun already bruised, ignored and hated by the new gods
unremembered by the old –
shining on our forgotten cities, fog-lashed, crowd-blinded
unsuspecting of these last, momentous hours
ridiculed by the tribes and bards, thinned out to bone
plagued, mosquitoed,
as we sit waiting for the darker hours
so we can go
and follow the remaining random, muted stars

All is in flight: the paper birds we made, dabbed with paint
glued up with mulch from flour, flapped past and are gone
the monks stole past – clutched book, bent yellow gait and page
and we, cursed by each frostbite
damned by each psalm or poem, impure
gather the animals and search for the other pasture
the next spring, some promise of flint, of porridge

All is in flight – left is the sound of nature's justice
the eternal jaws of the eternal chattering of ants

There was a cart, more of a boat inside a dream than cart,

that always prowed on, despite mist or cold, towards the
brilliant, fanciful city of our hope
the city which was unhaunted by the sights of all those cut
which was without the tear, the soaked bread, the shrill sound of
a shovel against a stone, metal on stone
the city which had our household, its wooden rafters fragrant
still, from a memory of root, its plants and horse, its air and kin
interplaying alongside the thresher who insisted she loved her
harvest and where each stone
marked the pathway of a dream

I have built the cart, twine and sackcloth, rounded wheel,
inside my soul
I am waiting for autumn's breeze, flap of a wing and song
and surge to my
untraded home and lands.

～

Restless rest,
the camels wheezing
gods hiding behind cliffs
and inside the thicket's tiny blossoms
the descent carved on each torn muscle
and then, the past drums at my temple

You have been my past
my body, my pulse
each image of you scalds the moon
that scowls at my remorse

The men will gather to wash the body
you never loved, stiffened by the retiring cells
leathered by the worm that snapped its spine
longing in my thoughts for you
without your veils and cloth
caressing the eyebrows clean of frown
the pubis clean of rusted hair

And you will weep

The women will gather around the shroud
with loosened hair, solemn on a solemn floor
and plait their sorrow against a silent wind
and you will recoil and cloister our past
And you will weep

The men will lift me up
the men will sway me over their heads
over each other down past these inclines
and devil-haunted, balsam-haunted, devil-conquered
paths to my mother – the sea
its azure and glitter and umbilical weed
humming my limbs to tender clay and ash
to send me off to Allah's marine gardens

And you will stand on the rocks
veil-waving, harsh, austere, serene
and between the eyelid and the eye
the wrist and navel, and inkling of a lecher's lore
And you will weep, oh you will weep and weep

And I will be carried off on the humps
of whales with red ribbons floating from their fins
rested, beautiful, in restless times
beyond the ache that garnishes each of my arteries
and bones

And you will, oh you will weep
for us, for me.

∿

Oh my love, my life I said
as I revived feeling my headless neck
and crawled past the mass of torsos, to the stakes
where the redshirts planted our heads
to frighten as they said the restless natives

I felt the wood the splinters, and despite the numb pain and the
fatigue, felt each head after head who spoke to me, asking for my
clan name and whether a Zondi or a Ntuli ancestor claimed me
as his own; and then with my fingertips searching past the dried
blood and onto my familiar neck, I stroked my face and opened
up my eyelids against the blazing Nkandla sun; I searched for
my teeth in vain; I lifted you off the sharpened tip and felt the
ivory earring gone and behind the ear, the war incisions crusted;
I placed you under my arm and said oh lead me out of this land
broken by infamy and barter and with my head under my arm
I ran to the left of the sunrise, my eyes, my tears, my heart, my
body still possessed by war muti and lioned, my legs, tired, but
still, zebra's stride of my praise name; I ran; and the mosquitoes
did not harm me; the Umfolozi crocodiles and eagles smile on
me; the valley of Phongola shrieked through their cicadas my
homestead's names; the Shangaan giraffe with its beady eyes
showed me the way; field-mice cooked themselves for me to place
over my torso into my gut; and the head under my arm cried at
nature's last call and mourning sound; the elephant did not hear
me; the wild cats bowed their heads in shame; the ibis and the
gwala-gwala shrieked at my sight; I ran; on the thorn fields I
heard the voice confused by the cross and the moon and the star
and the head under my arm cried, take me to Ethiopia, run dear
soul run, because it is said that Bambatha has run there ahead
with his head under his arm crying too; and the lakes did not
drown me, the people gathered on the paths and knelt, humming
in strange but familiar voices about the end of our worlds.

And I ran, the homesteads of men sprinkled me with water, the
rows of slaves tore at their metallic arms and I ran; my head full
of tears and my legs, ligaments gone when the sun, with a red
scar on its chin, laughed and said, those are your mountains, the
birthmarks of our clans, run boy run, lift your head above your
shoulders, decorate it with garlands and wash it of brine, you
will be home tonight, and I ran up the heartpath to the land of
the winds of time, my head high up above the shoulders to start
again the rounds of sorrow, homecomings, exile and the promise
of centuries of malcontent. Oh my love, our lives, our scars.

from **Rhythmskewed** (2000)
originally in Greek, 1991

~

You see, I was **born – a towncrier**, a tellalis. I remember: I was
one or two years old when I decided to scream out my handsome
words against the world but I couldn't, because they did not
school me to speak them in their tongues; instead, my lungs
swelled up with air and my sails swelled up and flapped against
my threads and linings, underneath the ribcage and the heart; I
found out too that my tongue could not rotate its lathe and my
poor words travelled up and down windpipes, found corks and
obstacles, so instead my sails swelled up some more, and more,
and more, so I exploded, my stomach linings and my umbilical
scar burst and my torso sagged into the tiles. So they placed me
inside red rubber beltings which tightened their grip around me,
so I cried from the constrictions.

And now, look, it is entirely their fault, I wander screaming these
spoilt words around these neighbourhoods and streets.

Childhood memories: the swelling of the sails, the tilt, the lifting
sensation, the sound of the first tare, the wind against bone, the
intestines dangling and red rubber belts tormenting my syntax,
my rhyme.

~

The house, grey, with a little courtyard at the back and its kind
shade and its concrete paving-stones; in summer the sun's mallet
pounded the rooftiles, and the lemon-blossom scents from the
yard's trees and the rosewater's from the aluminium containers
and the olives' from the clay pots, and the cauliflowers' on the
boil ("get out, out of the kitchen, out"), and the frankincense's
and the oil's aromatic wafts in front of the sombre icon-stand,
and the saints' icons marching up and down the corridor, and
the murmur of the aunts and uncles praying to St Fanourios (as
something was always lost or just gone missing) was my world.

And there: grandmother Eleftheria, wrapped in her shawls
and black attire, the general with the round-rimmed glasses
that glistened from the sun's flames would besiege me with her
fearsome armies – she, in front – close at hand, Kourkoulianos
("if you did not eat up all of your dinner") and all the others:
saints, demons, Laistrygones, Kalikantzaroi, Turks, English,
Giants and Pharisees.

Ha! – with arrows and a bow I would retort, smashing their
windows.

∿

I adored **the journeys** to the end of the world, on the waterfront,
on the promenade, there, where the waves smashed fish upon the
rocks and they would gaze at you with their stunned eyes.

My eyes were sore but keen, sprayed by saltwater, carried by
the wind howling all the way up from Egypt, my bacon pierced
by Poseidon's trident, my world playful from the sun's tricks on
the colour of ships, the sailing boats, and the fishermen's tiny
nutshell-jetsam, and in summer with outstretched hands I would
declare, the moon, mine, the boats, mine, their stevedores, mine,
and the scents from the kebab shops, also, mine.

The barber would shine his razor clean, bolt the shop's door, take
out his trumpet, and the festival would start.
And in winter, when the bolts of lightning spliced at waves, and
flocks of foam would graze the shore, the sky would hug tight
around my sweater.

I knew deep inside my heart that the wheel would turn once
more, and the dolphins and the sea-medusas of the deep, would
beach themselves to eat Odysseus because this island was mine
and not his Ithaca.

∿

"**Fire...Fire!**" – we could hear the voices, the tumult, the cries

I remember: it was the time of curfews and confinement, late at
night, I could frame through my window the glow, the colour
of ripe nectarines, shining at me from the Turkish quarter, its
intensity burning at the soles of my feet, numbing my arms, its
smell pressing on my lungs.

I remember: the elders pacing up and down the corridor, the
neighbours on their ladders, wall to wall across their courtyards,
murmuring to each other in whispers whose real purpose was a
scream.

The old women, I remember, making and unmaking beds, out
of habit, out of terror, out of madness, murmur – praying and
I, trembling from so much frost and so much fire, noticed that
all our heroes were beginning to lose themselves to tears just like
me.
Later I understood that we all knew the parts screams played
in the drama, as Troy's women tore out their hair and swore
blasphemies against their oracles and gods.

∿

The bravest of **superheroes**, the one who strung St George's
dragons and who slaughtered Mr. Droussiotis' cats; the most
revered of bodies, who sliced the chicken's throat before it
marched into the oven-pot, who fought against the waves and
the sharks that waves sometimes grow, who clasped at the jaws
of crocodiles was commanded to go, not to a hermitage, not to a
little country church for his confessions and earthly recompense,
but to the eating joint – where all the renowned fishermen of the
town hang out, reeking of sardine and musk.

And so, it came to pass that father and son, at four, in the
freshness just before sunrise, set out to devour the awesome
food of dawn: humus soup and after that, skewered meat and
meatballs, held by pig-testicle-skin, garnished with onions and
peppers in Homer's rose-fingered dawn, father and son devoured
the sea's body and blood and burped out, in satisfaction, foul
concoctions with fish dangling, sparkly earrings, from their ears.

~

Oh yes...
Born, on **ragged ground**, strangled by seas – the sky shoved at
the horizon, waters shoved pebbles ashore; mountains oozed
out their vineyards, grapes oozed wine and blood, blood of the
toilers, blood of Christ, bread His body – Eating and drinking
Him for centuries.
We feasted.

~

Born, where **Rimbaud's boat** crushed,sober, to supervise quarries;
in my town, in its public toilets near Zigzag street, near my
aunt's home – where another, the national bard of the land, was
employed to clean those toilets by municipal authorities – there,
in the vinegar stench of vinegar and wine warehouses next to
the haunting remarks of Zigzag street's whores, there, next to
the steam-world of Turkish baths, in its public toilets, where
Rimbaud, haunted by syphilis, agonised for relief, as the other
one cleaned the floors, near Zigzag street, in the very same toilets
– I found a map of Africa which rhymed.

I followed later, rhymeless and rhythm-skewed.

~

In the house, in its darker caverns all **the aunts** were spreading
their patience-cards and cracking the beads of their worry-
chains, stirring the pots of food sighing on the fire

The one wilting: a broken heart for her husband who walked off
and away, by now gaunt, diaphanous, a skeleton.

The other: with her French words and the dark shadows under
blue eyes, with her Cairo stories from the days of the good life
before her husband Harley Davidson-ed himself to death and
now, here she is in this bitter life, in this cursed town, clothes
always dark and sombre.

And in winter – when we were seated round the fire, roasting
chestnuts as uncle Aristides and grandmother Eleftheria
spun tales, they sat silent, distant, like the iconstand, they
would pierce you with their eyes, but their souls were floating
elsewhere, in some past, where the guitar's notes danced the
bolero through the night and where masked serenaders sung
erotic stanzas and life was rose and garnish; and in summer –
during the season of the mountain-cherry, and the watermelon
they would sip their bitter coffee, their Turkish blend, with
salted biscuits cracking, then melting in their mouths.

∿

The streets are clogged by **ancient Greeks** in trousers searching
for adventures and for fickle praise – with bank guaranteed
orders and loans, with traditions and historical tropes, over there
Mr Hesiod roasting corn cobs on hot coals and Euripides here,
sweeping the streets and Sappho with a cigarette dangling at the
soccer-tables and Aristides fighting with rows and rows of toy
soldiers on the pavement and Epaminondas hollering out the
numbers of the state lottery and the bank teller prophesying, a
new oracle, that Euklos erred: no one will be born again to sing
and spin divine odes; the only value will be conferred to those
who have a hire-purchase car and the old inns with their stables
still reeking of donkey will be closed and the stench of manure
will be terminated and Hector's story – Hector the mountain-
shaker and warrior, will be terminated, and neon lights will
illuminate the bitter, devil-battered, town's renaissance.

∿

They came from Kenya with their red berets after they skinned
the Mau Mau rebels, scorched their fields and killed Dedan
Kimathi right after Richard the Lionheart's crusade, with
their red berets, on warships, the best troops of Mrs Elisabeth
the queen, to teach us a lesson, to wipe the land off these
revolutionaries and the newspapers announced the great deeds
of these frightening boys with their redcaps, horrific and
courageous boys, and we all gathered at the seafront to see them

– to admire them, to swear at them, curse them and flay them with our eyes before they turned around to spike us – and the grownups recited Michaelides: "the plough thinks that it devours the earth but it always ends up devoured" as they arrived, row after row in their thousands and the seagulls howled and the trucks grumbled and the sullen crowds admired them – our eyes – the eyes of archers, our spite- arrows, but there was no earthquake when the bells started to toll – they came and went like all the others.

∿

Hundreds of Thousands of Years-worth **molecules are spinning** in my brain ancient sins, wines and massacres, plains full of soldiers and bone and that sky with its turquoise billboards soiled by smoke, by cloud, by the hecatombs

So many thousand molecules, shaped by history's rhythms – the molecules press, solid, visceral, at my brains and ignite ancient premonitions. There are dreams of copper, of swords and chains – copper chains of dreams that crossed from Africa, from Crete, on curved ships from Phoenician and Achaean shores and the endless rattle and the Assyrian dancers turn and spin and press at me and this sea, this humble and poor sea with a pair of tug boats – a sad solace – are calling out for my return.

We do not know whose life we lead during this night, we do not know which prehistoric rhythm we are dancing to, whatever we know is false. What you remember are the lost fragrances of thyme, the wine the screams and threnodies, and the crackers under the priest's aprons at Easter and a suffocating love and a parched life that only aches for water and the pheasants prophesying rains and thunderstorms.

One of those mornings, the sun, heating up the surf and roasting the coastline's piers, by the deep – where the shades of the seaweed lairs create a spooky undertow you could see in the distance, the fishing boat drunk, spinning around, on the same spot restless from the thickened wind blowing – thickened by salt-flakes and dust and sand scooped from the Sahara, each gust piercing pains inside all lungs; there too, the dead man from the neighbourhood around the corner was carrying his coffin to church as the patriarchs were fitting out their suspenders to prettify themselves and their women hanging up their earrings down their silky lobes – and the curfew sirens moaned. Dress up, walk up and down the corridor but stay inside, let the dead bury the dead.

I woke up from a dream that has been stalking me throughout the years, a dream that performed itself against a sombre, horrifying music: its scenery of ragged cliffs, deserted, arid plains next to a strange but calm sea and nothing else, neither life nor whisper echoed in its reel – a scene from some ancient prehistoric life, so obviously, a place of death, a space, where I to find it in my wakeful hours, my string would snap – a sombre, horrifying music of the future, the past, all intertwined round the mast of my soul. I woke up from it to find the harsh morning, roasting the surf and the seafront piers – and the curfew sirens moaned and moaned.

There – the little beast of the wild, the five or six year old – I placed the wind-up key inside the statues that were wandering aimlessly inside the house, I started to march them, row by row out of the corridor, out of the front door, carrying placards and olive and carob branches and their marbled feet kept thundering at the street's asphalt and I could hear the mighty wind's howl and din. Africa's Camel-wind was back, spinning and lathing odes inside my head.

from **The RDP Poems** (2004)

Black Mamba Rising

I

Walked
past Clairwood
and the back road
by the railway track
where the Local met
to change the world
and count who was alive

the building:
dirty-white as
dilapidated as it should have always been
the clothing sweatshop on the second floor
still, uncleaned windows from 1966
and the bare staircase
where we had to negotiate a wheelchair – three flights and a
twisted back
and a goat –
to cut its throat for protection
and eat it with the guys
the goat: still owns a stain
in the emptied hall
with its leaking lavatories

from the fire-alarm exit
the eye sees the only change:
a dozen women and their stalls by the
railway entrance:
one tomato, two orange and a piece of cloth

II

What happened to Qabula?
It is hard to get news, about Qabula.
The walk to the taxi rank, past Clairwood
to Mobeni might help:
asking his nephew, does not help.

He stares at you, and you can see the gun
on the inside of his leather-like, almost grey-jacket
surrounded by the guys who bleed the line from
Pondoland to the factory-gates
who serve the line, from the dagga plantations to Bambayi
taxi warriors who char the backs of HiAce scabs.
Tell the *umlungu*, he says, that I know nothing.

I drop the right names – his father's from Port Shepstone
his uncle's who died of the virus in Umzumbe
his friends' who fought the zombie-keepers at Kokstad.

Sitas, he says, I used to know you
through your words
but we do not know you, now
Qabula is my father now, since my father died
and he has the say of our inheritance
he is finished with your nonsense.

I lie about a film and money and
possibilities!

Capetown, he says,
looking for a job, you will find him
in Pondoland this Christmas
Now go to Hell.

III

Spoke to Mattera and he said,
let's speak to Mzwakhe
and to Kunene
you heard, we need to do something about Qabula
he has had a stroke. Paralysed.
Holy Cross Hospital. Bitter. Angry.
Nise said, we need to do something about his wife
she is on the brink of despair.

I push the CD inside the machine

and there is Mbuli's voice declaring
peace on KwaZulu Natal; but the real
voice? Vodacom. cell-phones

Walkietalkies – Mzwakhe-man
you have been stealing sugar from our tea, man?
Redistributing cash from our democratic banks?
We need cash for Pondoland, man. Could you help
at least for now man? No chance – they froze me up!

IV

Telephone wire.
My words faster than the people cutting it
off the phone-line, copper wire good for trade and craft!
My words make it, survival of the swiftest –
"Hello. uMi,lo?
– Excuse me sir, I do not understand
uMi ,lo?
Your director, uMi, man
You mean Mr Michael S'dumo Hlatshwayo!
Yebo.
He's busy. Phone again, next week
Can I leave a message?
I am afraid, I do not have a pen handy sir
Fakofu.

V

"Hello, ma"
Quick word past the copper pliers
uNise, she's there?
No she's gone.
Where?
Dead.
What dead, are you crazy?
She was on hunger strike and died of complications
What hunger strike? I was with her yesterday!
We were all together, yesterday, sir, but today?

Why didn't she say to me she was on hunger strike?
Oh she left a note with your secretary sir.
Why was it not in the Press?
You tell me sir, you are the intellectual, after all.
From now on, call Ms Sibotho

VI

uMi, man
quick word past another set of pliers.
Yebo, mfo.
We need money for a coffin and money to get to Qabula in
Pondoland
We are frozen man.
There is an investigation
into 3 million unauthorised cash
I don't even have a salary for this month.
We only have a small budget for Tourism

VII

Hello, Sawubona, Dumelang
Welcome to Durban
We are here to please and smile
we can do poetry in your room
give you souvenirs of our smiles and scars
we can dress dashiki or leopard leather
to maskanda or mournful howls
show you our lovely teeth
our words can gumboot through your brain
our mambas rise or crawl at your wish
welcome to Durban
we poets know how to smile at our keepers keep.
I will personally take you past Clairwood
where we used to meet and count
who was alive!
Love you all, love you all
goodnight.

Reconstruction

Working in the debris, I rescued a hinge
and then found another off the piles by the gate
and felt that something was lacking
as I stumbled into the cabin through the caking mud
and the tufts of green, weeding the path

On that first night I played with them –
like puppets' mouths between index and thumb
clacking to the rhythm pulsing
the wailing reeds on the stereo
and felt haunted by what was lacking there, still.
In the morning by the shed
at the pile of bones my sculptor friend gathered
– so much bone left in the fields
he used to say, where the animals get cut,
and cleaned them off the marrow and grime
to work, to work,
I chose two sets, roughly similar –
giraffe or camel, whale or ape –
who knows these days?
And, like an osteo-grafter I set to shape
and connect each set with the hinges
creating elbows.

And it was good.

Sleep that night was short,
too much dream and mist
restlessness and spleen and
after the fruit-bats bolted
at dawn and
the flies lifting off the greening haze
invaded and
the farms
around the estate with the dew's revived stench
as if perverted flocks of oxen flew low
depositing their dung and more,

I dismantled the broken sculpture
a Cuban doctor left with us
and took its frame of wattle
smoothed its edges, carved better the sockets
and created the frame and shoulders
for my moving arms of bone

To make the hands was sheer exhaustion:
two electrical twills fitted as wrists
around the bone
and in their groove
the base of old marionette hands
we used to make during our drama days
their supple fingers and their gracious twist
strung through with copper wire
pulled tight around the bone pieces
to a point through the centre of the shoulder-frame

I felt those frail and vulnerable limbs
outstretch, beg and chastise with subtle grace
and was excited
running to the sea, panting, puffing on the pathway
to the water, dark, angry smacking
its sparkles and
little cataracts on rock.

Far simpler was to craft energy and motion
A crude, three-stroke motor
with its ascent, deny, yes, no, yes, no, logic
could be battery propelled and ran through wire
to bring the limbs to life.
I refused the humiliation of corporate cells
and set about
to place a spine on a chair
and fixed the frame
and placed the system on a double-converter
one: linked to solar panels,
stealing sunrays for the pull and shove
one: linked to an aluminium box,

inside it – a fluid of chemical reactions
a kind of stomach if you please
to process organic food or mulch
and at the end of the day,
trembling with excitement,
handed life, animation,
motion over to my beautiful new friend

The box was busy working through the night
digesting, creating a hearth on the porch
for all creatures of the night to gather
I had to chase a scorpion off the frame
and then,
sampled sounds to construct
a humming,
chattering voice to blend in with the gestures
of the limbs
added a sadder loop, a frail crescendo
an operatic voicing for the dying of the solar rays
during the rain or night
and another loop, more blues and pain
as the aluminium stomach
ran out of feed and timed it
to my friend's arms
and their cadences.
Oh the last day was pure fever:
first the stockpiles
of bone produced a vulnerable
cranium for a head
I wish I knew it was a deer, or goat, or camel
damn it, let it even be a dolphin skull I moaned
what do I know of metaphysics or zoology,
jagged and cracked;
glueing all kinds
of padding to the frame
I unfurled over the head, like a soft condom
her skin
over her shoulders
and breasts

through the arms and all the way past
the metallic stomach and waist
a skin crafted through thin hemp
and although it tore by the jawline
and chest, the right elbow and fist
it added to the frail beauty of
my friend

Then came the red dress
and the touch of charcoal and paint
and the draft and dab
the lines of fine features.

When she murmured and sang
to my gathering friends
the day after
— my wits and street fighters
my friends who sell and buy
the ones who play witness,
the survivors who dream
the drinkers and thinkers and eaters of swine
of nectar and blues
they all roared in approval and named her
-Beatrice
-Isabella
-Nandi
-Sita
-the Beautiful unborn
and teased and coaxed
lit cigarettes and placed them in her mouth
and she murmured on and on and struck such notes
of anguish

I chased them
I hated chasing them
I had to chase them
past the gate
and returned to look at her,
alone

in a love beyond
a senseless new
landscape of
reconstructed hope

Living Rites

1

Farewell
in a small hall
where the sister
insisted in agitated
breath
that the coffin
was to be opened
after the gospel reading
—You do not get AIDS
by looking at the dead

2

The body is the
little dormitory of pain
ruined
in silence

3

You see
mumbles the minister
searching for soap
to wash his hands
no Indians came
making some serious
political point

4

Out there:
past the fake
decorations
spreads the habitat:
copulating

defecating
by the river
infecting
exhaling
scalping
people have become
some problem

5

Half –
dying to be exploited
Another half –
killing not to –
in between –
the in-transigence
of death

6

Re-member:
all this
was bodies
with untold pleasure
on a soft, soft mat
or a hard goatskin
all this was grounded

7

Does the festival
of Africa's rebirth
the drums that code
the secrets
the heartbeat
the frenzy
raise the dead?

8

The long struggle
of the antigens
— haggard and paler now

a heap of viral furies
in the rooms
lifting and losing
the excesses of love —
is almost over

9

The foothills
and the meadows
the dreamlike mist
the beautiful
DhlomoPaton-ted landscape
of the river that kills
of the cloven hoofs that
waste the cattle
The shit in the pig trough
luminous waste from the urban bog
The inhale exhale of the
intimacy of man, woman, beast
The thousands in their lines
sharing a drip

10

Steady drizzle
The woman drenched
dejected
stands offering
to some ancestor
her fault
that she couldn't
test the virgin status

of her young

11

The dormitory
is ransacked
from the remotest
corners where even
geckos refused to hide
to the paltry living room
There remains:
the wince
the grimace
the effort
the chest-pain
the thrush
the tortured breath
the rancid smell of some
concoction
in an emptying space

12

Raffled skirts
and a sackcloth sari
sweeping the earth
a placard:
the poor will not
cannot
must not pay their rates

13

We march
we, of the virtues
we, of the devotions
we of the dedications
we who serve those
in pain

all of us marching
one back, one coffin
one coffin, one back
into obscurity

14

Farewell
the pulse
the movement
that has shaped me
is driving by.
Fast.

Times of deliverance

When the cloud-cover passes over
     this five-rand town
searching for respite from the wind that goads it
past the moon
&
the tarmac – warm
from the day's subtropical chore –
yearns for the landcrabs and frogs to return I know
that this is the place where language must have died

where memory banks declare certainties in
undigested drones – oh yes, and
tremulous voices
heavenly choirs
briars, pyres
scraps

(stop that shit, collect copper wires)

Dear keeper
     I am a communist because I recall
crabbed songs,
frogged rain,
       I keep the calendar on a green page

Hello Mr Grief
here comes my goofy sorrow
Hello Mr Poet
Grief here, have you some tear
for me to borrow?

There is an open fire
where the trail ended
and the spoor calcified
where some mongrel-snout prows its longings
past some unwanted spume
in this four and ninety-nine plus one cent place

where the tongue used to twist-lash in timed
constrictions

Hello Mr Grief
here comes your tear to borrow
Hello Mr Poet
Grief here, at what interest
does eye-liquid, sorrow?

I am a communist
&
    keep the calendar on a green page

Seated here, naked in the
chemical compounds
of this damp afternoon
that masticates the wings of tiny predatory birds
listening
          to the chipping of ozone granules
behind the dark beards of cloud
I try to clone the nano-particles of
feeling on this war-torn sitar

oh the roads we have built boys
oh the droughts we have mitigated
oh the books we have almost balanced, boys

"One came back, hid the gun and waited
another wandered the streets, disco-scatta-talking to himself
another robbed a bank and then another bank
another wandered the countryside, cracked heart
half-dead torso the rest was moved by wheelbarrow
cursing
another found the gun the first one hid
another drowned searching for a tap
the third paid for the posh coffin of teak
the fourth turned worm and hired out the wheelbarrow to taxi
the one who scatta-talked pushed it

and the new one with the gun took it
so we crawl through the thicket
listening to the trucks delivering all of us
off our basest needs."

Oh the roads we have built boys
the books we have balanced boys

Hello Mr Poet
here's sorrow
Oh you are very welcome Mr Grief
tomorrow
has been mortgaged
you are stunningly free to borrow

oh boys the droughts
boys

and

the
trains...
trains:
     ...gravy
       stains

Lament for the Dying of the Word

1. The poetess who died, whose funeral it was; provides her monologue first: she describes why she killed herself by refusing to eat and therefore inflicting untold complications on her frail body. She describes how she decided to join the pained indifference of the landscape.

2. Twenty-one crying, hired comrades sing their sadness, falsetto voices, about the power of spirits and the strength of communities to overcome.

3. The Minister who knew her best, who only on rare moments of the heart abandons his scripted speech, abandons his scripted speech and speaks from the heart about the land of the mend and glory.

4. The Zen poet who had nothing to do with the narrative, felt compelled to enter the proceedings, since he was attending a poetry festival nearby and sprinkle tiny diamonds and little clumps of silicon dust over the graveside.

5. Ten dogs arrived to apologise for not sensing death, when she approached, but take the opportunity to complain of feelings of low esteem and how they have been traumatised in the townships and the suburbs. What will become of us, they whimper, when all the fences go?

6. Her latest poetry book reviews itself. It is a hesitant and reflective account of recent declarations from critics who own the means of persuasion: apparently they had persuaded somebody, somewhere, that work like hers was out of joint with these anointed times.

7. A feminist leader intervenes to castigate the constant monologue of men, their talk of viper tongues hiding behind their kindly smile. You haunted her throughout her life, you haunt her still.
You haunt us still.

8. The presidential office sends the wrong message by mistake. It chastises leaders of other states for failing their people.

9. Her first lover declares that he was her lover and now, even if he warms up a very esteemed position in the administration of the arts, he is saddened by the loss of touch from the tropes that made the grassroots sing, their younger days to sing; he offered above his sorrow, the creation of a special Trust in her name.

10. The second lover, carried around in a wheel-barrow, dejected and paralysed, launches into a tirade against the first. Against his betrayal, against his uppish ways, against his illusions that she was in love with him. He does not see anymore a poet of the masses but a skin and bone bag of coins jangling in the street. Only he, the betrayed one, could be her soul-man beyond the tears and the pain.

11. At which point, lover no.1 and lover no.2 berate each other about the mutual discovery of their affairs. The exchange unfortunately, plummets the standards of discourse to profanity.

12. From all the nooks and also the crannies of the earth, the planet mourns for her. The spirits that were hidden by ecclesiastical pomp and circumstance, the older spirits, upset by observing women pounding yam and praying to God, sprint through each crevice to claim her.

13. John Coltrane arrives to mourn for her, his love boundless, his prayer screaming, his saxophone a tunnel of despair and glint and grief. Ayler moans back, and there – Leroy Jenkins cuts the strings of his violin and Mingus tears the mood out of a cello and Toure fingers a guitar each time Tobejane smacks his skins. Swim they say, across enchanted rivers.

14. A Chemical Engineer has people in raptures with his cloning miracles. He clones back into life all the poets since Rimbaud and Mayakovsky and clones too back into life all the subjects of their obsessive, metred love. The chorus of bleating babies,

tagged with the appropriate names fills all the lungs with hope. They shall return when they learn how to enunciate and speak. The loved ones will return and we shall buy shares in their copyrighted genes.

15. A third lover intervenes and to the greatest consternation of the gathering declares that he was also, indeed, a lover. The greatest discord is that he is a white man who claims to have decided to come out to challenge the taboos that kept their love life secret. To the hissing of the crowd he displays photographs of their intimacy and love.

16. Lovers no.1 and 2 turn on lover no.3 and it is evident that they were all part of some culture local.

17. Mahatma Gandhi arrives as usual to save the situation. I have been lost in the forest, he says in an apologetic tone; I have been confused by slide-rules and calculators but I am back to reclaim the ground that needs reclaiming.

18. One hundred cellphones ring in tandem. They all echo, like some epiphany the voice of Mzwakhe Mbuli singing about peace in KwaZulu Natal.

19. Our sociologist makes a timely appearance too, to provide a class analysis of the conjuncture. His student assistant, displaying the overhead projections, is rumoured to be a recalled sangoma and an industrial psychologist. All she has to do is hold the sheets right up in front of her eyes and the image firms and forms in earnest over the podium.

20. An imbongi bursts through the crowds orating in a language no-one remembers.

21. The most beautiful woman on earth walks through the crowd. She stands on the platform and squeezes out a tear. The crowd sighs.

22. The people arrive in their thousands to sing and sing and sing while the oxen drag the carts with the mountains of flowers, her books and belongings, her kettles and pots and pans, her brooms and computers, and of course her crafted coffin into the ground. Bellowing can be heard from the earth's deep tunnels and lungs.

23. A slogan sings itself. To infinity.

Bombing Iraq

Come,
come in
Welcome to my little show
Mind your step
Don't touch the props
Don't touch the piano
I know it is not tuned
Leave the animal cages alone
And don't touch the beautiful cattle-heads
They are hard to make
Don't talk to the ghosts in the shadows
They will have their turn
Here are the maps
This is Iraq
The buckets of sand are for your toes
The meat on the table is real
Don't eat it, it's raw
We will get to char it much later
Please, some respect
It takes years to gather such metaphors

∿

Draw the dark
Curtains
Place
The moon up high.
Light it. Talk to it.
Dribble a string of red
From the edge
Of its wet mouth
Get to the shower-head, boy
Pelt us some rain

Look at these dancing legs
This-that dancing
Look at my fiddling thumb

Worn to the bone
Draw the dark curtains
Switch on the noisy tape
Gunshot, firework,volcano
Let it come:
Blood, ovaries, solvents

Let the animals loose
Let the meerkat or leopard, boy
Pace about
In the thinning light

Dawn-stalker
Beach-sand stalker
Curse you, sun
All I can offer you is my skin
To burn

I share the seagull's impatience
Her tiptoe
On fishbone
On the leftovers from the revels
Of the night before
From the scrapped pianos of the deep
That rhythm-pulse at waves
From the lungs
Of the stalking ibises
Trumpeting soprano shrill
"hay-de-ho"
the ibises
trumpeting tenor-shrill
"hai-de-dah"
on the shore
announcing you
in the cloud-free morning

Curse you sun
Africa's traitor
Faminiser

Flooder
Droughter
I have had my fill
Of umbrellas
At the lines of aid queues
Counting the wilt
The crack
The cuttings of the daisy –
Cutter bombs
I have had it
With the burial cloth
The burial climb
The hymn
The shroud
On this sun-infested landscape
The stretch of hands
Counting the bacilli:

Bombing Iraq

෴

And there:
A gaggle of prophets
In the costume store
Already rehearsing some auction
Some price

"Oh Lord,
you have become so
necessary
We flock, we clerk, we follow
The brass band, the majorettes
Oh Lord, your signature
Burn me a bush, a tree
Strike us, harm us, incite us"

On the path,
The goats chew cans

Drink dew
And I walk in rhythm
Mangled mind, kitted body
Singing against the choirs

"(I'll be glad when you're dead) you rascal you"
crooning
*"I'll be standing on the corner high
when your body passes by
(I'll be glad when you're dead) you rascal you"*

"Oh Lord, strip us
traffick us, pig us
you have become so
necessary"

By the home for the homeless

"burn me a bush, a tree,
pig us"

by the termite mound
where witches roamed so free
the gramophone bleats, the rope
tightens.

"(I'll be so, so glad...) you, rascal, you"

"Oh Lord, we flock
fashion us an amnesty at last
incite us, strip us."

The dowry, confiscated
The errors, damned
The darkness, harnessed
The lice, deliced
The pockets, filled
The goats, sacrificed

"Oh Lord, we clerk
we follow, we rehearse"

*"standing on the corner high
when your body passes by,
I'll be glad, so glad.. you rascal, you"*

By the goatskins, the prison wall
Refracts the moon
Pure cricket and bat
Gaggle, gaggle
Prophet, price

"Oh Lord, your greed
your wrath, your giggle
pig us"

*"you rascal you...(Oh I'll be glad when you are dead)
you rascal you"*

All we have left:
An elephant's trail, perhaps
And I walk in rhythm
Mangled, kitted
To kill:

Redemption.

᷍

On the seventh day
I surrendered
I simply ran out of glue
Ran out of the flour to make the glue
Ran out of water to mix
The flour to make some glue

I looked at the pieces of flesh

The torso, limb, liver, shin-bone and could
Do nothing
But history knows I tried
At least, for six days.
I tried

I swear
And she is my witness
That I persisted
That I did glue the pieces together
And set them off to march
Again
And at night, as you know
The bombing would start
Each strike the better, designed so much better
To tear it all up

And I would start again:
3 cups of flour, 1 cup of water and mix
to glue the new pieces together
even if I was short of shards,
of hands, of toes, of sinew
again and again

I tried my best
As long as they managed to march

∿

Remote control: click

My son
My son
Which is your skull
What was my sin

Remote control: clack

So many blondes
On TV
Whisping around
Guitars –
Romantic
So many plaits
Strutting the stage
Guitars –
Romantic

click

My son
My son
Which is your skull
What is my sin
Which pile
Which mound
Do I start from
My son?

clack

∿

Look at the photographs

They danced those girls
Danced
One of them: my mother
The other her friend: another's mother
The third too.

Not knowing that later
When their graces netted men
They would have to follow
One: to Tanganika; the other:
To Johannesburg; another, to Baghdad

To tie their graces to a chore
And leap across protected pantries singing

"Three little maids from school are we
Pert as schoolgirls well can be
Filled to the brim with girlish glee"

Look at those young girls moving
they danced those girls
in kimonos, by the swan's lakes
the photos are there,
as they shuffle
heads buried in their huddle
in their three-way shoulders
searching for sons
in some unspecified wards.

∿

Unlike my elders
I cannot ask who piled
The mounds of coke-cans
And the mounds of skulls
In this darkening space
I know this room.
I know who brought them here.
The wheelbarrow is still poised
In the dimming, sun-freed light
And in the darkness over there
I cannot ask after the clicking sound
I know
I have met the dark-clad aunts
I recognize their kitting
The dead have time
Knitting,
Knitting,

I know the mounds are dented
I know what life has passed through here

The clues are everywhere
The piano is still warm from the pummel
And the cross-hand rhythm it endured

And there:
Those are the last remaining prison bars
My poet friends peddle to survive

The mounds are there
It was a monumental effort
That rolled them up the flights
of stairs.

∿

The pods he used to rattle on his ankles
And the leopard head he used as head
Have been hung
By the piano by the shacks
By the thatched
Vodacom umbrella
But everytime he felt the spotlight
Warming his face
He jigged a rum and coke-stop to a tango
To soften up the chores

"They still need to faint away their scraps
next to the aluminium heaps
so I give them Cuba"
he said

Unlike most others
He still had fingers
To frighten off
The snakes that nestled
By the chords
Inside the soundbox
Inside the soul.

∿

I was troping Ethiopia, bra
He shouted
I was swinging a bottle
Moaning the Moors
Painting the gutters blue:
Loss-this, loss-that
Loss-that, loss-this again

Blacken me with sugarcotton, bra
He shouted
Blacken me
Ma weaned me
Cooked me vleispap in the sun
But it is all bloodJah, bloodbra, blood
Swinging the bottle, moaning the Moors
On my guitar.

∿

& was love possible
you asked?
Apart from explosions
A good story needs a love-affair

I don't need you, she said
I don't need you, I said
Both caught in the drought
Stuck in some soundtrack, cracked lips
Smeared lip-ice
Life's enchanting straps

Me: circling Mecca
Circling Auschwitz
Counting the trees
Outside historic fences

She: rose in her teeth
Thorns in the gum
Proud to escape
Some knife on her clit

Was it a ship,
If ship, no sails, if
Track, strange sounds
Westering, northing
Who knows

But I know what
we scratched on each other was real

And if I was to thrust my shoulders
And if you were to shake your eyebrow
And if I were to gas them
And if you were gassed
And if I were to walk through your eyes
And if we ever got lost in a land of true feeling
And if we mistook each other's for Allah's brow
And if we wilted apart
We would still never be loved

〜

I long for you, she sang
Tara-tara
The tremor in the voice was French
The tune was boomslang venom
She sang

I will spare you the car-chase.
(it is enough: explosion, love-affair
are sufficient for our purposes)

"I am your halfwaywoman as you
are my halfwayman"

Nothing is
Like it was before, she sang
Tears well up at the tight-shut door
Knives strike stone, stone shields
What used to be some ore, the tremor
In the voice was French, the tune
Was boomslang venom
And she sang

"I am your halfwaywoman as you
are my halfwayman"

No my love
We are not here
We are in Bombay cutting Moslems
On Gandhi's road to Ahmedabad
We are slaying the cows
Roasting the lamb

Bombing Iraq

No, she sang

I will spare you the car-chase

"I am your halfwaywoman if
you are my halfwayman"

ᗯ

I protest
I have paged through your latest brochures
And I am dissatisfied
Because I have come to demand my rights
My democratic choice

I protest

about your cluster-bomb that spreads so wide

To maim the entire street
Mixing my own with my money-lender's
ribcage

I am dissatisfied
With the post-napalm, vapourising shit
That burns so slowly after the first grimace
Raising a collective howl

I demand
A post-shock, post-awe
Personalized bomb
I demand ideological consistency –

One person, one necklace, one fire

One, customized, singular seepage from the final charred mound

I protest

about the daisy-cutter too
Which does not distinguish
Between a child's stem and mine

I demand my own sensual stamen
My own diversity
My own discorporation.

∿

Draw dark the curtains
The faminiser of a sun is creeping in
Draw the dark curtains
Silence the izingisi-bird
Fake some peace, at last.

RDP Film Documentary (RDP Project Launch, Inanda 1995)

Interview: You scaled the fence?

Observation: taut,
unbarbed wire
surrounding the Municipal Dump

– The fence could be scaled
but the guard
raised heavy blows
so my trickster voice
said to my head,
work him,
work with him
so now I sleep inside
next to the shed
and hide
my shopping cart
inside that bush

Observation: squat guard
irritated, fanning himself,
some flies are out to eat him

– That guard is nice
he only takes "the VAT"
two rand a load
they pay them shit, you know
and has a kraal of many mouths
to feed out by Sipofu

Camera: wide shot of the dump
past his left shoulder
focus: flies,
focus: the colours
of the decomposing mulch

– First come the birds

the fat ones with the engine-voice
later, five to ten minutes
come the thin ones
with their bounce and kill
and chase the fat ones
and they wake me
so I start to load first
the flat irons
at the bottom
then the tubey ones and then
stuff the gaps with little ones and wire
and leave the bulky ones to pile on top
just like a bus, I tie them with this rope
I have to work fast
because the day guard comes
and he is not my friend
then the squatters from Fastrack
Cato Crest
and Jamaika
come
to fight the guards
over the piles

Camera: focus on the thin,
toned and nerve-jerked arms
the chin close to the chest
as he heaves:
the imperative to show the effort
the bumps on the side-road
the traffic
the metallic clatter of the wheels
the struggle
the imperative of craft

– There are 110 times 100 steps
from here to Sydney Road
ask these hardtimed shoes

The first ten times a hundred steps

lorries upset me
arrogant drivers
force me off the smoother grey
and it is sandy and bumpy on
the side
weeds creep into the wheels
so I call these steps BEWARE

Camera: close up of the junk
the cart
the wires holding up the rickety piles

– A heavy manhole cover is the best
makes the kilos dance right on the scale
a head of a lawnmower is good
a fridge or stove is also tops
a car door, man, a car door
if you have the cutting tools
railway lines are a celebration
awnings
exhaust pipes
machines
that board there with the map
God dances up your spine
you shake a wing
and you are in heaven!

Camera: the lorries and trucks
the concrete mixers
building the hospital
the strange early, mechanical stillness of day
the empty soccerfields
the board he wants to cut:
"RDP project area"

– Oh all the steps
20 times a hundred there
 the river next to the road
to Chesterville

then another fifteen times hundred
the bad turn where the SPCA was
then Manor Gardens
and then Ethusini hill
the pain hill
the UP and UP, the Khalo Hill

Camera: fences, dogs barking
focus: teeth, bourgeois aggression
on the poor
Pigeon Valley, caress the thicket
show the face
by now his mouth: open
a sign of dry tongue
show the Glenwood
cornucopia
radical angle-shift
Industrial Sydney
Remember – the soundtrack has
to change

– Tired after Sydney like the land
after ten years of the sun
standing still, each year a rand
I take the R10
a beer,
bread and polony
a cigarette
and save one rand
I rest and light up
at the park

Camera: caress the
stretched-out body
and fade to
child singing and selling
a tomato by the park

from **The Book of Accounting**
(2008)

feel the
restlessness
of debt
— most debts are hard to settle

the eczema from a bearded nettle; the unrelenting eagle's
shriek; the orchid's poisoned petal.
the pain of the worm in an egret's beak; the tug of a hyena's
jaw.

DEPARTMENT

Summer Love

I couldn't help her die
That summer,
Oh summer,
Oh summer love

Dying in Durban is harsh in summer –
preening mosquitos, from the thick soup
of bygone larvae, strike, siphoning blood,
where blood has become scarce, where life has become scarcer,
as the dampness, creeping
through the leaves, the stalks, the green,
implodes lungs hope and desire

Winter at least hangs a kinder cloud –
it gifts the CD-count some respite dreaming of a square meal
– sweet potato, garlic, olive oil and beetroot –
even though sardines did not run this winter
the oily scent is from us,
swimming about, cooked, tinned, canned

It was in February then, when death yields a dividend in stock
When you and I dragged ourselves to share
such an imperfect beer

And you said hold it right there, I am not a Zulu I am from
Griqua East, pure Hotnot – as if that mattered

At least the counting was in English: your CD-count OK?
– and visa versa: OK.OK.

My father let me ride the refinery truck, back on the farm.
The same BP kind that hauls olive-oil from the harbour to the
shacks. We smiled and sipped yet another imperfect beer.
Hold me, I have the shivers. This heat... This, heat.
The smell of the grease in the joints of the haulage cranes...

Let's walk the mulch of the low tide, peel off your shoes
Let's talk about the coral.
Perhaps…talk about rock paintings.
…Immortality.

∿

Hey kid – leave the wallet alone, padded with business cards
You can't trade them in for glue
This place needs more than glue –

You have a knife, I have a gun, now stammer me a dance
Hey kid, you are trembling, I see, this is alas, a vengeful,
relentless sun
"La ilaha illal Lah wadah, la illaha illal Lah….
La ilaha illal Lah wadah, la illaha illal Lah.."
Pray that my index finger knows something about clemency
Dance on, kid, remind us why I need you dancing
in this heat? This, heat?

No this blue umbrella is just for us
Come – under the blue umbrella dear

Hey kid, I am teaching you the basic rules of art
I expect gratitude, remorse what holds
this nightmare together is not glue
but fear – fear and antigens
but mostly fear and vengeful, relentless toil

You like the way I spin the shaft of the umbrella, she said
I was the golden, their golden, drum majorette girl
At Kokstad High I was the queen, I was to be a model by sixteen
When we get back, I will let you cup my breasts,
the thrush is killing me

Let's hoist the yellow flag

∿

She loved ballroom dancing

∿

There were also briefings at important hotels
The imitation Corinth column behind the toothshine
porter with the purple sash – shabby sash, shabby sash, shabby
sash, shabby…the origin of salsa
Tretchikoff tear down the wan, wan face, smudging the canvas
Drank tea
Heard briefings
In teacups made in China, spoons made in Benin
Like Dingane to a Shaka, treason claims one more headline
One more deadline

The neon-candles steel each face, the ceiling fans
unfurl the puffed out wigs
 Plastic bamboo trees in water features in the lobby
Ifuku – a state of tangled green, a state of nature
I had to run for air

Threw up,
threw over the wrought iron balustrade
onto the guard's dog
Debriefed

∿

Look at this diamond stud, a boyfriend gave it to me once
I want to bleach my hair, she said.
Shall we go to the movies? she said
He drowned, she said
Who?
My boyfriend
Springtides will bring him back
Don't call me Hotnot.
Yesterday you insisted I called you Hotnot
That… was yesterday
What would you do if he returned, all wet and longing?

I am an ordinary girl, she said, two abortions
and a 5 year old living with my mom, the usual stuff
The doctor and the nurses hinted at complications
Time is very, very tight.

I imagined her boyfriend –
The hull from some wreck in the deep scraped his fins
and misted his snorkel
And then, the brine, brine
Something leaps off the foam.

The boom-box, struts a boom and a thud and a soft roxy bleat
Big Beat
To Ithaka. To Ithaka. Home
Ekhaya. Ithaka. Home.

In between: Buddha is dancing
Another virgin blows herself up
In Palestine

Dancing

Buddha Dancing

Ballroom dancing

ᔕ

The scent of oil from the can in the bin
the smell of grease from the haulage cranes
brine
a cell phone ring-tone, a demented parakeet
Hanuman waving from the window pane
Can't find a yellow flag
A yellow MTN-bag will just have to do
It will not be your boyfriend
The cinder of the bygone war
Antennae are waving CNN salutes to Al Jazeera

If you love me you will bring that pillow to my face.
Tight.

I could have never loved her
that much,
that summer.

Oh summer,
Summer love

Jazz, Bass and Land

An improvisation in memory of :
Johnny Dyani   Elson Gcwabaza   Siphiwe Khumalo
Mazisi Kunene   Ramolao Makhene   Max Masango
Martha Mkhize   Ingoapele Modingoane   Alfred Qabula

From Johnny Dyani
to Commandante Hani
An era ends
Since then it's money,
money. Money.

There… on the right: the Navy band all pomp and brass
they jita-bug
There on the left: the Shembe horn-men, poly-scalar
Wheeze-in, blast out
My friend Futshane with a bow guts the double-bass low
Wherever there is music, there is hope
The phrasing is Dyani's, from Biko's Song to an
Angolan Cry, the restless dead intone.
Faster than the wind
We are sleeping home tonight.

The bassist moves to the left and starts his tribute to Dyani
slow, controlled, promiscuous,
it hums into the eardrum, it plucks at the inside of the stomach
slow, controlled, as language fails each octave
each slide, each pluck.
You expect Moholo to rain on skins and cymbals
He is not there.
You expect Abdullah to place his left hand on the keys.
He is not there.
But from the left, taut, the guitar-man fiddles
pure maskandi, pure pele-pele, pure Madala Kunene fingers
circling on the strings, as if he left the streets
and is really talking to the stars
They meet to greet each other on every 16th pulse
Leaving the listener one breath short, a heartbeat far behind

as they are talking about some Mecca
or some spiritual den.

At that, my ethereal friend
Don Cherry gets his break on the cornet:
Crystals exploding from Timbuktu to LA
each screech or squawk shatters the peace
dragging the bass, stretching the chords to counterpoint.
This is the language between madness and rebirth
The final circus act of a tradition

Before the brink, the pianist brings it back
Yes, yes, Melvyn Peters – dreaming Coltrane
earning his dough from tourists who demand more crap – eases
the ear, upbeat-swing so low and merry,
tonality returns, redeems
and Dyani's bass responds pure cheek, pure wily nigger.

Oh no, Sazi Dlamini will not be outdone
and back from his Kunene-astral grooves

swinging chord and yoke, shining smile and blue
the Navy band breathes back to ooze
the Shembe horns awake to breathe.

The bass responds
The big band soars and quietens
Leaving the trombone man alone
To grunt and exorcise the ghosts
The ugliest horn on earth, sheer chain
and joy
it obliges: even the ugly, love.

But no, who let Ngqawana in?
No build-up but a cataract – aggressive wails
burning his lungs while squealing each three beats
to pause and scream some more at something no one sees,
at something... everybody feels

The chaos calls me, can I sing?
Where do I find the pitch to say and improvise my string?
The mike is trembling, Dyani, Hani, here we go
here is the sting – the tabla, drum and cello, guide me in:

Privatise the Sun
Copyright the Clouds
Before those others come
To steal our Rainbows
From Johnny Dyani
to Commandante Hani
An era ends
Since then it's money,
money. Money.

from **80 Days Around the World – the India Section** (2010)

Mooring

Harpooning the angel was easy
Tugging him down to the dhow,
mending him, to nail him to the mast,
was hard
Unfolding his wings to steer
against the crosswinds through the Arabian Sea
through Ratnataka was
sheer joy

So we sailed

Past floating mines
Past the coast-line with its oil rigs on fire
We saw what effendi Rimbaud saw: azure swells, cruel moons,
harrowing dawns, unforgiving suns, where, flotsam-pale,
ravished, drowned and pensive men float by
Gibreel, Gibreel, we shouted, stick to the saffron side of sea
The Green is dangerous

We saw the ships draped in cotton and raw silk
The arrogance of Tata banners and flags
Their Filipino crewmen tossing watermelon rinds
To hungry sharks
and the red eddies, marking the graves of slave ships.

and we corked by
the last game-fish
wrapped in pashmina shawls
followed by fishermen with bait, with hook and sinker
and sticks of dynamite

Ahoy Land!
Gibreel, Gibreel stick to the saffron side of sea

The mist lifting its skirt
To an indifferent grey
Where are the Himalayas? Where is Cochin?

The captain brought out the maps, the compass,
The GPS, soggy Jules Verne's pages,
Soggier biscuits

Ahoy, Mumbai!
Brought down the mast
Folded the wings
Loaded the cameras, the SimCards
Easing the boat

Ahoy Gandhiland's shopping malls
Behind the Gun Boats
Behind the Gateway
The Taj on fire!

Master and Slave Dialectics

-You are stupid
-Yes, I am stupid
-No, *I* am stupid
-Yes, you are stupid Passepartout
-Stupid to have followed you
-It is my stupid charm
-I didn't even need the stupid money
-You don't have to follow me stupid
-You'll tell the boss
-Don't be stupid
-How will you manage without your slave
-I will sit and pine for you
-Who will be your Tweedle-dum to be a Tweedle-dee?
-I will miss you
-I will catch up
-Catching up will be hard for you
-Who are you going to insult each morning?
-Oh I forgot India has run out of people
-Why do you want to get rid of me so much?
-I had enough of your blank stare out of this window, you
are wasting metaphors!
-I will catch them on the way back
-It doesn't count you will see them in reverse
-What's there to see?
-Your Elephant-man, the Magnifique he's been riding on his
bicycle
next to the train – there!
She looked.
-Stupid.
-Ouch.. that hurt
-That was my left hook, you wait for my right

I could not understand how she could have had a blank stare.
– Just crossing India in an AC2 ticket is grand enough. Just
knowing that you are in one of 45 796 coaches, welded together
at Integral Works of Chennai, and the Rail Coach Factory of
Kapurthala, being pulled by one of 7 612 locomotives pummeled

together at Chittaranjan Loco Works and the Diesel Works of
Varanasi, or Diesel-Loco Modernisation Works of Patiala –count
150 000 souls hammering and sweating, and that there are
another 17 999 trains out there this moment travelling, their
wheels turning because of Rail Wheel Factory of Bangalore in
one of the 8 984 passenger trains, being served by one of 100 000
servers, and behind it all Mittal Steel and Metal pumping out
billets and rods, and behind that miners digging pig iron or iron-
iron, or ferrous and non-ferrous rocks to pound them and smelt
them at 1 800 degrees Celsius thank you very much and over
there at Aurangabad Siemens is setting up and GM is setting up
and Bombardier Canada has already making metro coaches in
Vadodara and exporting them to all and, get a perspective here
what your arse is sitting on!
-What?
-No! All you are interested is on your stupid boyfriend from
Bombay riding on a Chinese bicycle or tricycle next to the train.
-Where?
-There.
-Merde. Here comes the right hook.
-Ouch that also hurt. And this is a window. You are supposed
to look outside at the tilting horizon, the relentless sun – at the
fields, at the peasants, the bullocks, the dhania and chilli plants,
at the palms and the nutmeg and clove, at the wheat-fields, at
the scare-crows, at the peacocks eating the seeds, at the peasants'
bungalows and the kids playing cricket with planks of wood, at
the temples, at the jungles, at the tigers and the sad elephants,
there are 1 billion souls out there not counting animals, insects,
viruses or bacteria all waiting for you to look at them!
-Why?
-Because you have a window-seat. You can get off in
Aurangabad or Burhampoor – that's where the Thugs will get
you and strangle you – that's where they poison politicians.
-You sit here, come…you just missed a metaphor… too late.
-What?
-We are not stopping at Aurangabad – hey look: that's a baby
Taj Mahal! Look: that, I swear is Karl Marx in a silk sari – look
at the smoke, Insulin, Siemens, Beer, oh my it's saffron smoke,
even the sulphur is Hindooized. Didn't Karl Marx say so?

126

-What's the metaphor, stupid?
-He is wearing a silk sari.
-What will I do without my slave?
Burhanpur: the ancient trading post of muslin and silk to
Bagdhad, Istanbul, and even Krakow. The citadel of the Bohras
and of the ancient pilgrimage.
A grubby platform:
Passepartout's eyes: diamonds.
At the entrance: Chinese bike – Monsieur Magnifique d'
Elephant waving an asbestos-caked hand.
-What will my slave do without me?
-Ellora, Ajanta, the Caves, Mumbai, lots to do stupid
-That was not the question, stupid!

Learning to Love
(after Faiz)

Here:
Some beads for the wave of your tresses
Bead them in hard, shiny
against the jetblack of your greying hair
Slaves were traded for them, fingers bled to thread them
They shine – little colourful skulls
Of the Day of the Dead from Mexico
I come from far, here: the beads
Plait them in the jetblack of your greying hair
So I can learn to love you

Here:
Some tears for the dimple of your cheek
Run them slow, shiny against the narrow of your chin
Infants were killed for them,
palms were leathered to collect them
They shine – sun-struck crystals
From the saltpans and the pampas
I come from far, here: the tears
Rain them softly against the narrow of your chin
So I can learn to love you

Here:
Some soot for your brow and lashes
Texture it in deep, a dark henna against your haunting eyes
Outcasts were starved for them,
joints were cracked to scoop them
They haunt – tiny mirages of the desert
From the pit bogs and the crags of the equator
I come from far, here: the soot
Craft it in against your haunting eyes
So I can learn to love you

Here:
Some red pearls for your ears
Hang them low, crimson treasures from your softest lobes

Naked divers lost lungs for them,
eardrums exploded to collect them
They pulse – little ripe pomegranate-seeds
From the reefs and the swells of the Red Sea
I come from far, here: the pearls
Pierce them through and hang them from your softest lobes
So I can learn to love you

Here is the soft pink for your lips
Smooth it over, soft and aromatic scent for a future kiss
Jews and pigs were boiled for them,
chemists lost their skin for them
They entice – the madness between a heart and flower
From the vats and cauldrons of the subcontracted East
I come from far, here: the soft pink
Caress it on softly, an aromatic scent for a future kiss
So I can learn to love you

Leave your breasts bare
There is no mindless youth or loot to hide there
Leave them just there
Just there
    So I can learn to love you

Remembering Freiburg

Swart trees in a darkening Europe and the icy wind on the paths
of the Swart Forest by Freiburg.
Hexenloch
The sun refused to rise or set for us
Prof Martin Heidegger walks ahead in mountain boots
and shorts, donning a hat with a feather.
The whole city breathing the essents he bequeathed to it, the
hills are historically stuck with his hikes.

How good was Hannah Arendt in bed? Herr Doktor Professor
and why did you cut poor Edmund's stipend?

Why do you walk the midnight walk of all the attics still –
your ghost-step firmer as ever than Weber's? I am trying to
understand what of your sentences sent Marcuse away, my
granddad to the ovens.

As you said, to know is to stand in the truth

To restore man's historical being-there
To read Holderlin by the cow-shed

To be inconsolable about the collapse of Munsterplatz to a
multikulti Markethalle; to be stern about Martinstor bearing a
McDonalds burger-hat.

The totality of the history allotted to us! He bemoans
The heritage of Western Man!

Who are you? He frowns, who sent you here?
Ich bin der Schachautomat, nur Kraftwerk und
TechnoGuevarismus
Ich bin your worst Uberscheisstraum – which of your sentences
sent my granddad to the ovens?

Is Being a mere word and its meaning vapour?
Are there techniques to vaporize Being?

Are there words to describe it, Herr Doktor?

Are there too many Turks in the street, sir
Shopping from Chinese 1-Euro Shops?

Do you still yearn for the venture of demolishing the world in
the name of the authentic?

Here: Hexenloch where the shimmering ice
wrests being from appearance
There: the Schwarzwald Panoramastrasse picnic site.

Have some slices of Walderschinken, sip a Graubugunder, sir.

The essent has become an object – he bemoans; don't worry sir,
the essent has become a digit and a DNA repeat.

The object invites observation or transformation into a product,
he bemoans or a calculation, he shrieks. Don't worry sir, the
world is fractal. Epiphany has died, he shouts and nature is
reduced and vision has become mere optics!

Oh spare us your vision Professor Herr Doktor, spare us, our eyes
are fine, pathetic man.

Allahabad

It was important to have a conversation with
Pandit Nehru in Allahabad
After the visitors left the fine house
We sat down for tea
Overlooking the confluence of the sacred rivers
I marveled at the variety of trees

-So Pandit how is the dream?
-Fine. Stronger than ever: even when we lose, we win
And when we win, we win. It was a dream, now it has its
emanations
-But the dream is declared a nightmare by many
-Look at the trees. Each tree has at least four post-modernists or
what do you call them? : post-colonials chirring. They face this
way and they are lambasting the dream. If the dream goes they
are gone, there is nothing, all is meaningless.
- How so?
-It is right that the Communists strive for revolution – CPIM
– they think it is right and we think it is right that they are
wrong. Take the Maoists, they think that the dream stalls
the revolution, it is right that my friend EMS thought they
were wrong and it is right that we think both are wrong. Take
the dream away, they are nothing. It is also right that the
communalists strive for Hindutva and it is right that we think
they wrong. Take the dream away, they are nothing. Should I
talk about the Dalits? It is right that they think the caste order
remains, it is right that we think they wrong. This is dialectics:
the dream is both the space and time for the molecules to clash
and shape.
- The Congress is not where you left it, Pandit!
- It either serves the dream or doesn't, that's all.
-What about the woman who sits under a tree at night crying to
the heavens?
-We cry with her.
-What about the squalor, the misery, the utter disregard for the
spinner, the plougher, the weaver, the child that dies at 14 from
overwork?

-They were the reason for the dream.
- So all is well?
- Better than ever. India is real. Even if we lose, we win, the dream is both the essence and the existence.

The two women wafted through the streets instead in the company of a dishevelled Nirala – to get provisions for the train-ride to Bengal. They came back with no toiletries, hampers, dresses or shawls. They returned with poetic metaphors instead: chrysanthemums, spinning wheels and shrouds.

Time to leave Triveni Sangam as the crickets in the ancient trees start chirring industrial policy ragas.

Varanasi

The train stops at Varanasi.
Behind each silk a suicide
Behind the cracks abandoned handlooms
Spiritualism lurks, in each nostril burning tyre
Rickshaw-men tout and hassle
to pay back loans in Ayurvedic banks.
And yet, something lives on
In the caking mud, in Ganga's sulphur
In-between decay and obstinance
and barter

The officer, more plump than muscle
Who spoke of terror all this way
Turned soft and breezy on the platform
Heading for Sarnath for a deep mystical chore,
Bade us a mournful farewell
She took a pearl right from her eyes
and placed it in his palm
And he was gone

Untiring crowds
Officious holy priests
So many bodies
Burnt, the lines are long in heaven
On the short-cut to some eternal bliss
And Hori's Cow lost between incessant horns
And chants
The sun dyes the river red
Raising a pink sliver of a moon
There is still hope
Symmetry, desire
On the shelf of a makeshift shop
In between, the Vishnus and the Shivas
A Buddha is smiling.

Kolkata 2

There was a pavement
By the Hospital for the Dying Destitute
There was a crowd
She said, bye-bye madman
I felt her hand slip out of mine
A last look in the eyes
And she was gone

There was no way that I was not to find her
She was the journey's
Destiny and its conclusion.

Oh Kali, fiercest Kali of Kalikata
Protector of the hearth
Godess of strife
come

The streets of Kolkata
Defy pain
And the contrast between melody and noise
is so stark that it defies sensation
Kali it is your turn in this cosmic mess
To break the harmony

I would like to hear beyond the melody
which you respect to such distraction
I don't sense your feelings coming through
the perfect symmetry of notes

Oh Kali explain to them
now
BBD Bagh, Chowringhee
Howrah Bridge – the noise, the push-carts and bullocks
Chalo, chalo, chalo and the infernal horns
Break through hymnodies and songs

How do we move beyond the drone
Away from the eternal essence
But the discord, the draining
Impatience of movement, chalo, chalo, chalo

All 200 ragas that you've learnt are false
Their notes and playful cadences – falser
The charisma of great sound is the grand excuse – falsest
Pure treason
Hosting mahfils is feudalism's revenge
Gharanas – sites of repression

Was Hanuman ever a Naxalite?

How thousands of years of civilization
crush each time a dalit speaks unfettered
each time she speaks, what if she sings?

A wounded civilization, Kali?
Never:
It wounds.

Kokovoko

We did not find Kokovoko
You promised, said Passepartout
Sometimes fiction cannot cause reality, I screamed
Sometimes? she asked
But you did promise me: "Kokovoko"

I did.

And in the hours of tedium she sang
Ditty after ditty about her prince from Kokovoko
Who would steal on us and take her on his fancy-wood canoe
In the moonlight he would take her to the coasts of Orinoco
Where the silver fish of Chavez flow downstream
from the Andes upland-highlands of Peru
or she would disappear in endless rhyme-games
of Kokovoko, koko, loco coco, yoko anything to free me she
would moan from the constant, daily, you!

But we did see the whalers
We saw how they were struck,
how they were killed and how they were sliced and cut
And even saved a Greenpeace volunteer
From wave and shark
There was nibbling but it could have been
An eel or something nastier but never the jaws of death

It is beautiful tho, she said,
That we are here and not
Like them
Like the thousands on the shore
Needing each a penny for their ocean reveries
Or the Andaman islanders
removing salt flakes with tiny tweezers
to free their land from Tsunami Jo's unasked-for gift

I wrapped her in seaweed hammock,
hoisted her up, eye-level

twisted her around until she hang unmoving
and explained the basic rules of craft-oil, blubber and sperm.

"You whale and me Ahab" I said.
"Here – inside your head would be your junk: particles of oil,
thousands of oilnests or pimples."
"Exactly… we have more bone to oil."
"It's your tits or your bum that may be more generous."
My fingers over her head and behind the neck, "there…*that's*
where most of it is: the oilsperm…it is soft and wobbly…
becomes hard jelly if exposed… thousands of litres of sperm.
You look pathetic you are such a useless mammal."
You promised me Kokovoko!

How good the drink
How light the heart, how gay our jokes our maps
Here: Scheria where I would find
my Nausica to help forget Aouda
There: Lilliput and next, look at that Haleakoloa!
No to the right! Dr. Moreau's islands!
How quick-witted were our repartees –
That's Bali Hai…no…no, too low…, these are dangerous waters
I can see Pala… and just as the wind picked up again
Shivering from rum or wine, nodding in deep yogi
understandings – we are doomed to never, ever see it:
Utopia, there and the wind damn it, nudging us away
Metaphysical and nasty winds always keep us away
Why does the wind boom against the ropes, shouldn't it twang?
How deep is the depth of this bottomless sea?
And when the wind turned to howl,
When waves dashed aboard and the squall trumpeted
Parades of sea-horses
Instead of the fire and crackling, the eerie silence,
cocooning the storm
Before the carnage
To speed us off course into Reality

It has been a long voyage
The brine has caked the joints

And the hands are too weak
to open the glass jar
our species of sputum collected on the road
will have to wait another day
And I stand in this bracing wind repeating the Ramanama
To excise ghosts
Yearning and ready to endure silently
more horse or human kicks

Come to Macondo then on the 81st day
Where all – Negrito, Proto-Australoid, Mongoloid,
Mediterranean, Brachycephal and Nordictypes are welcome,
including people who share and do not share a hukka and where
Nayadis and Namburis may dance
in the torpor of a tropical noon.
It is pointless reaching London
The San Francisco harbour has Four Large direction signs:
One- Arrow Back: back where you came from, will rather eat the
card rather than green it for you Punk.
One-Arrow Left: To Ice and Exotica and if you persist, Alaska.
One-Arrow Straight: London
One-Arrow Right: Home. Macondo, 7236kms.
You have gone crazy, Passepartout smiled – It does not say
Home
There is no Home.

from **Insurrections** (2012)

Tune in

too tired to march
too neat to hollar
a weak to bellow
snot by the stacks of solid waste
snowed our little finger. Pa.

The sky smelled a little that night
made him fear to queasy
that night.
There was a crescent moon
Thickening, shoes, naming leaves
we were hungry

cover illustration

we were hungry

Ghosts of the Quarry: Insurrection

Too tired to march
Too weak to holler
Too weak to bellow
We sat by the stacks of solid waste
And moved our little finger: so

The sky cracked a little
We ate lime from the quarry that night
There was a crescent moon
Throwing stones, waving banners

We were hungry

Too tired to march
Too weak to holler
Too weak to bellow
We sat by the stacks of solid waste
That's where they shot us

We are the ghosts
of the quarry
limestone of crescent moons
and at night
hauling buckets of stiff phutu
through your dream
: insurrection

Insurrection: Flowers

It started from a butterfly spinning
Once
Spinning twice
Dropping dead

I cannot remember lightning or thunder
All I remember is the lull –
Waters stood still,
The drop from the leaky tap stood still
A pearl without a chain in midair
Before the flowers burst the ramparts

The homestead surrounded
The cities besieged
The trucks, ambushed
The hostages, taken
There was blood
In what they called the insurgency of the flowers

They were everywhere
Leaping from vases
Snapping free from bunches
And there:
Flocks of jasmine
Murders of hyacinth
Parading up-down the emptying streets

The rumour spread to the trees
And they bloomed
Roses conspired with almond blossoms
The dangabane flower resurrected
The kunjiri blues intoned
And the secret ones of Qatalamba
Of Himalchand
marched off the crevices

In the arsenal:
The Orchid, arrogant
With a halo of
Humming Bees

The Eighth Insurrection of the cow

I stabbed the foetus
with these
I used to stab the rain with these
How did you dare
grow this inside my womb?

Exchanged for the hyena
To in-laws
with sharp knives
Cut at the dawn by gutters
Whose water ran with slime
My girl was roasted
Where maggots sing the street
Where maggots serenade the moon my dear
I stabbed the rain with these

My white patch takes to flight
my dear
uNala was my name
Inala was my regiment,
I was too a makoti once
the cwebezela one
what shines my dear
are only stars tonight
like bats, they drop to me
I stabbed the rain with these

You hear me bellow dear
You're wrong – I ululate
Where you have seen fine rivers
And valleys full of cud
I have leaked and scorched
my dear, the pathway to the dead
is faint to see

Broken the pen my dear
Run flat the kraal
Cried by the stacks of fillet dear
Poisoned the fields
Snapped at the yoke
Refused the branding iron
Sucked up my teats
And eight
I stabbed
with these

I used to stab the rain with these

The digital image
fold as the TV screen ti

E.

The cops, rifles in cabinet, past their third beer
are edging
towards bed

The
cabinet
the
smelter
has
been
closed.
the
only
music
is
the
wind
on
razor wire

from **The Vespa Diaries**

Klerksdorp

"I pulled into Nazareth
was feeling half-past dead"...
The Band: "The Weight"

Pulled off the earphones and yanked the goggles off to see
The waft of grey
The kranz and dune by Klerksdorp
Dressed in deep-yellow dirt
Like a deposit of grime off miners' fingernails
My eyes were sore
I scratched them raw

Took Half-foot to the township clinic
(picked him up 100kms back)
Nurse 1 took Half-foot in
Nurse 2, took me outside to light a Texan
"You have grey eyes" I said
She grinned – when people die here they all turn grey
AIDS scrapes off the black.
You HIV? I asked
Nah, she chuckled: too ugly even for the miners
This is more of a whorehouse than a Dorp
Miners get tired of each other in Auschwitz over there.
Your name?
Thembeka

Met the doctor, fidgety white
In his bare room jars with pickled lungs
Research, he said, Science, Cure, Death.

Rode back thru Prinsloo Street
And dismounted to find a blanket by the hardware store
"What does a good man fetch here?"

I asked the 10 foot farmer by the rakes
"A good man?" he pondered
"500 Rand but don't bring me a local *nie...*"
His wife ran a B&B
His wife ran the Hardware Store
His wife ran all.

"Strange" she said, "a blanket?"
"We have blankets plenty... just sign here...
Breakfast full English, Farm or Moffie?"
"Moffie?"
"Croissant and jam and paw-paw."
"I need a blanket to look up at the stars
Need a strong something
The strangest brew and a helmet
To stop their golden tips
From raining shards on me".

A Greek? fok! He exclaimed and repeated, fok!
That said it all: one worse off than a Jew!
You are a poet, she said
They come here often or come nearby to Ventersdorp
Looking for the story of Taung
And wet their pants!

She walked me past the portraits of
Eugene Terblanche, Phil Masinga and
Gert Schalwyk
And who is that?
Arrie Paulus she said, he was the hero once.
You can hear him sing at midnight
By the shafts
By the ghosts of the shafts
By the deep, deep shafts

I'll give you a blanket extra
If you take me on your Vespa
she whispered,
I want out
I said no.
There was this K-girl left a message
She said,
That Half-foot,
Let me get this right:
Will be No-leg
Diabetes ate it all up to his bone.

Everyone has a chink of gold
Lodged in a joint that hurts here,
said Thembeka,
breaking off a piece of star
dipping it soft
into the steaming tea-cup
you can have this sky dear
I'd trade it for a blanket or a Vespa
or a heart.

Evening Song (Durban)

After a day of stoning and gas
an ancient chore beckons
by the ocean's lip –
a crowd heaving, heaving, sifting through the sand
for coins
A happy bulldozer resting
after eating up another row of shacks
its jaw nestling by a crab-hole

What a fine evening
What a sea, what pulse
of insects
tiptoeing to the lovelorn strings
of a dune's cicada
What a toptiptoe of tiny birds
Hurrying in and out of pollen
before the blooms shut shop
what a sigh from the darkening mangrove
as the crowd picks up the evening song:
"musa ukuthath' investments ezulweni/
kodwa/
ukutheng' iLotto ithiketi/
thathani MaChance! uLotto machance!"

I cannot sing
A jagged bamboo knife has scraped my throat
To sing and remind whom what?
About the stars
or the strings of mango inbetween my teeth?
About the sneering palm tree?
About the piece of cloth waving in the breeze
on the barb of the casino's fence?
How the descending sun wrestles with the shadows
of the thousand hills?
How past dreams lurk there?
How no one remembers that they do?
How there is a residue of dream on my frown?

The night's very restless inyanga is already by the pier,
eyes shut, pacing
and murmuring the 11th commandment of a new faith
The beer-stained guards have exhausted their shift
umpiring since dawn the eternal struggle
between mynahs and crows by the rubbish bins.
The fishermen, past their third bottle of cane
dream of grunters, reek of shad
and complain that no ship was hooked
even though they cast their lines far in the far gardens of foam
And there: the sea's eylid full of fins
The factory sirens quiet at last
The hooligan moon peers over the Bluff
and the horses of the deep get restless.

In another time this would have been
the moment for our story-telling friends
but they are gone
Tonight the ridge and hills will not be on fire
The spring child's last sigh will not be recorded
The salt march will not pass by
The salt – yes, only the salt endures, the salt

I tiptoe past the bulldozer
Its eyes are moist
Dreaming of its earth-mother
In some abandoned iron-mine.

Marikana

The digital images fold as the TV screen tires
The cops, rifles in cabinet, past their third beer
are edging towards bed
The night is quiet as the smelter has been closed,
the only music is of the wind on razor wire
the ears are too shut to hear the ancestral thuds on goatskin
humanity has somehow died in Marikana
who said what to whom remains a detailed trifle
the fury of the day has to congeal, the blood has to congeal
I reverse the footage bringing the miners back to life
in vain, the footage surges back and the first bullet
reappears and the next and the next and the next
and I reverse the footage in vain, again and again in vain

The image of the man in the green shroud endures
Who wove the blanket and what was his name?
There are no subtitles under the clump of bodies, no names
stapled on their unformed skull
A mist of ignorance also endures, a winter fog
woven into the fabric of the kill
The loom endures too, the weaver is asleep
The land of the high winds will receive the man naked
The earth will eat the stitch back to a thread
What will remain is the image and I in vain
Reversing him back to life to lead the hill to song
In vain, the footage surges back
another Mpondo, another Nquza Hill, another Wonder Hill
the shooting quietens: another anthill

My love, did I not gift you a necklace with a wondrous bird
pure royal platinum to mark our bond?
Was it not the work of the most reckless angel
of craft and ingenuity? Was it not pretty?
Didn't the bird have an enticing beak of orange with green tint?
Throw it away quickly, tonight it will turn nasty and gouge
a shaft into your slender neck
And it will hurt because our metals are the hardest –

156

gold, pig iron, manganese
yes, platinum
Humanity has somehow died in Marikana

What is that uMzimu staring back at us tonight?
Darken the mirrors
Switch off the moon
Asphalt the lakes
At dawn, the driveway to the Master's mansion
Is aflame with flower, so radiant
from the superphosphates
of bone
of surplus oxygen and cash,
such flames, such a raw sun
such mourning by the shacks that squat in sulphur's bracken
and I wait for the storm, the torrent, the lava of restitution
the avenger spirits that blunt the helicopter blades in vain

these also endure: the game and trout fishing
of their elective chores
the auctions of diamond, art and share
the prized stallions of their dreams
their supple fingers fingering
oriental skins and their silver crystals
counting the scalps of politicians in their vault

The meerkat paces through the scent of blood
I want it to pace through the scent of blood,
she is the mascot, the living totem
of the mine's deep rock,
the one who guards the clans from the night's devil
she is there as the restless ghosts of ancestors
by the rock-face
feeding her sinew and pap
goading her on:
the women who have loved the dead alive
the homesteads that have earned their sweat and glands
impassive nature that has heard their songs
the miners of our daily wealth that still defy

the harsh landscape of new furies
the meerkat endures –
torn certainties of class endure
the weaver also endures: there –
green blankets of our shrouded dreams
humanity has died in Marikana

The strike is over
The dead must return
to work

Printed in the United States
By Bookmasters